High Employment without Inflation

A Positive Program for Economic Stabilization

A Statement on National Policy by

the Research and Policy Committee

of the Committee for Economic Development

July 1972

Shambaugh Library

Single copy ... $1.50

Printed in U.S.A.
First Printing July 1972
Design: Harry Carter
Library of Congress Catalog Card Number: 72-86317
International Standard Book Number: 0-87186-047-3

Committee for Economic Development
477 Madison Avenue, New York, N.Y. 10022

Contents

The Responsibility for
CED Statements on National Policy

This statement has been approved for publication as a statement of the Research and Policy Committee by the members of that Committee and its drafting sub-committee, subject to individual dissents or reservations noted herein. The trustees who are responsible for this statement are listed on the opposite page. Company associations are included for identification only; the companies do not share in the responsibility borne by the individuals.

The Research and Policy Committee is directed by CED's bylaws to:

"Initiate studies into the principles of business policy and of public policy which will foster the full contribution by industry and commerce to the attainment and maintenance of high and secure standards of living for people in all walks of life through maximum employment and high productivity in the domestic economy."

The bylaws emphasize that:

"All research is to be thoroughly objective in character, and the approach in each instance is to be from the standpoint of the general welfare and not from that of any special political or economic group."

The Research and Policy Committee is composed of 60 Trustees from among the 200 businessmen and educators who comprise the Committee for Economic Development. It is aided by a Research Advisory Board of leading economists, a small permanent Research Staff, and by advisors chosen for their competence in the field being considered.

Each Statement on National Policy is preceded by discussions, meetings, and exchanges of memoranda, often stretching over many months. The research is undertaken by a subcommittee, with its advisors, and the full Research and Policy Committee participates in the drafting of findings and recommendations.

Except for the members of the Research and Policy Committee and the responsible subcommittee, the recommendations presented herein are not necessarily endorsed by other Trustees or by the advisors, contributors, staff members, or others associated with CED.

The Research and Policy Committee offers these Statements on National Policy as an aid to clearer understanding of the steps to be taken in achieving sustained growth of the American economy. The Committee is not attempting to pass on any pending specific legislative proposals; its purpose is to urge careful consideration of the objectives set forth in the statement and of the best means of accomplishing those objectives.

4.

1. Voted to approve the policy statement but submitted memoranda of comment, reservation,
   or dissent, or wished to be associated with memoranda of others. See pages 62-75.
2. Did not participate in the voting on this statement because of absence from the country.

Project Director

FRANK W. SCHIFF
Vice President and Chief Economist, CED

Advisors to the Subcommittee

WALTER W. HELLER
Department of Economics
University of Minnesota

CARL KAYSEN
Director
The Institute for Advanced Study

ARTHUR OKUN
The Brookings Institution

DON K. PRICE
Dean, John Fitzgerald Kennedy School
    of Government
Harvard University

ALBERT REES
Director, Industrial Relations Section
Department of Economics
Princeton University

CHARLES L. SCHULTZE
The Brookings Institution

HENRY C. WALLICH
Department of Economics
Yale University

CED Research Advisory Board

Chairman

CARL KAYSEN
Director, The Institute for
    Advanced Study

EDWARD C. BANFIELD
Department of Government
Harvard University

ALAN K. CAMPBELL
Dean, The Maxwell School of
    Citizenship and Public Affairs
Syracuse University

WILBUR J. COHEN
Dean, School of Education
The University of Michigan

LAWRENCE C. HOWARD
Dean, Graduate School of Public
    and International Affairs
University of Pittsburgh

CHARLES P. KINDLEBERGER
Department of Economics
    and Social Science
Massachusetts Institute of Technology

JOHN R. MEYER
President
National Bureau of Economic
    Research, Inc.

ARTHUR OKUN
The Brookings Institution

DON K. PRICE
Dean, John Fitzgerald Kennedy School
    of Government
Harvard University

RAYMOND VERNON
Graduate School
    of Business Administration
Harvard University

MURRAY L. WEIDENBAUM
Department of Economics
Washington University

PAUL N. YLVISAKER
Professor, Public Affairs and
    Urban Planning
Woodrow Wilson School of Public
    and International Affairs
Princeton University

Associate Members

WALTER W. HELLER
Department of Economics
University of Minnesota

FREDERICK C. MOSHER
Woodrow Wilson Department of
    Government and Foreign Affairs
University of Virginia

CHARLES L. SCHULTZE
The Brookings Institution

HENRY C. WALLICH
Department of Economics
Yale University

Foreword

THIS policy statement presents a basic reappraisal of the causes of economic instability in the American economy and proposes a program for achieving high employment without inflation. The timing of the statement and some of its recommendations were prompted by the New Economic Policy and the need, several months after its adoption, to assess the implications of this major departure in the country's approach to economic stabilization. The fundamental reason for undertaking this study, however, was the recognition by the Research and Policy Committee that in the current economic environment, monetary and fiscal policies alone could not achieve the nation's stabilization objectives.

Given this Committee's predisposition to avoid interference with free markets, we have traditionally taken a strong position that appropriate fiscal and monetary policies are the key to economic stability. Our January 1969 statement on *Fiscal and Monetary Policies for Steady Economic Growth* and our 1970 statement on *Further Weapons Against*

Inflation reaffirmed the central importance of these policies, while proposing that they be supplemented by structural measures such as institutional changes to make labor and product markets more competitive. The 1970 statement also included the recommendation that voluntary wage-price policies be included as a supplement to monetary and fiscal policy and structural reform.

The positions presented in this statement are consistent with those taken in the 1969 and 1970 statements but go beyond the earlier proposals in emphasizing the need for a positive program to bring about the necessary structural reforms. It is our view that this type of program offers the best chance for creating the conditions that will allow fiscal and monetary policies to play the predominant role in achieving economic stability and growth. In this context our recommendation on standby controls, which is clearly the most controversial, may well be less important than the other more positive recommendations.

The present statement deals with the general framework and direction of stabilization policy and with the particular steps which need to be taken. We recognize, however, that definitive answers are not yet possible for all of the questions raised by the recent unsatisfactory performance of the economy. For this reason the Research and Policy Committee can be expected to continue to evaluate the future course of inflation and unemployment, as well as the recommendations made in this statement.

I should like to extend the appreciation of the Research and Policy Committee to all the members of the subcommittee which prepared the statement, as well as to the subcommittee advisors. Frank W. Schiff, CED's Chief Economist, deserves special recognition for his contribution as Project Director to the background research and drafting of this statement.

Philip M. Klutznick, *Co-Chairman*
Research and Policy Committee

1.

Introduction and General Conclusions

THE NEW ECONOMIC POLICY initiated by President Nixon in August 1971 constitutes a major departure in this country's approach to economic stabilization. Its most prominent feature is the addition of a system of mandatory price and wage controls to the more traditional arsenal of stabilization weapons. The result is a greater degree of direct government intervention in specific economic decisions than has hitherto been considered appropriate except during periods of supply scarcities accompanying large-scale wartime mobilization.

We believe that very forceful action had indeed become necessary to cope adequately with the twin problems of inflation and unemployment, and that the Administration's program of wage and price controls deserves the nation's broad support. But we also consider it highly important that every effort be made to assess the new policy and its pattern of implementation in broad perspective.

More specifically, there is a need to focus on a number of basic questions: Do the recent steps represent a set of temporary emergency measures that should give way to exclusive reliance on more traditional stabilization instruments after a relatively brief interval? Or must the country become reconciled to more basic changes in its approach to stabilization policies in order to attain its major goals? If the answer to the latter question is affirmative, does this mean that a significant degree of reliance on economic controls is likely to be required for some time? If so, how extensive and permanent would such controls need to be and what form should they take? Finally, to what extent can improvement of the structure of the competitive system be used to achieve non-inflationary high employment with a maximum of freedom for private decisions in the market?*

Answering these questions adequately calls for a basic reappraisal of the forces that have brought us to our present situation and of the full range of economic policy instruments that are currently or potentially available to cope with the country's stabilization objectives. For the Research and Policy Committee of CED, which for the past thirty years has been deeply concerned with developing rational approaches to the achievement of economic stabilization, this reappraisal has involved a searching reevaluation of policies we have advocated in the past.

The present statement presents the initial results of this reevaluation. It does not imply that definitive answers to all of the questions raised are as yet possible. Rather, it is concerned with the general directions that policy should take as well as with particular types of action that ought to be given priority attention.

Although this statement focuses primarily on domestic policy issues, we are fully aware of the major role that future international economic policies will play in an appropriate over-all stabilization strategy. Should such policies lead to persistent balance-of-payments difficulties and increased restrictions on the movement of goods and services, capital, and technology, the efficiency and dynamism of our economy would suffer and domestic inflationary pressures would be intensified. Liberalization of international economic policies, on the other hand, can be of direct and continuing aid to the domestic stabilization effort. The basic policy stance in international trade and financial matters that the United States takes over the next few years is very likely to have a significant bearing on the prospects for greater economic stability, both at home and abroad. Many of the international policy issues that need to be faced have been covered in our November 1971 policy statement on *The United States and the European Community*.[1] We plan to deal with other aspects in a study on reform of the international monetary system.

---

[1] *The United States and the European Community: Policies for a Changing World Economy*, A Statement on National Policy by the Research and Policy Committee, Committee for Economic Development (New York: November 1971).

*See Memoranda by MR. ROBERT B. SEMPLE and by MR. ALLAN SPROUL, pages 62 and 63.

The Challenge of Reconciling
High Employment and Price Stability

The principal aim of stabilization policies is the attainment of high employment without inflation in a setting of steady economic growth. Traditionally, the main tool for achieving these goals has been the use of fiscal and monetary policies to influence the aggregate demand for goods and services. But since inflation can be fed by cost-push pressures as well as by excessive over-all demand, efforts have also been made to supplement demand management with other measures. Up to the time of the New Economic Policy, these had included "structural" measures to render labor and product markets more competitive and, during some periods, voluntary wage-price restraint involving a limited degree of direct governmental influence on particular wage and price decisions.

The experience of recent years, however, has raised doubts as to whether these various policy tools, in combination, are adequate for meeting the essential policy goals.

The most important doubt stems from the fact that the application of the policies has by and large failed to produce really satisfactory results. Even more important is the fact that the gap between desired and actual performance rapidly widened in the period immediately preceding the introduction of the New Economic Policy.

As shown in the Chart on page 12, there have been very few occasions in the past two decades when price increases and unemployment were *simultaneously* held down to reasonably acceptable levels, such as the "interim" targets of about 4 per cent unemployment and no more than 2 per cent inflation. These were the targets cited in official statements over much of this period.

During most of these years, however, inflation and unemployment tended to move in opposite directions. When aggregate economic activity strengthened and unemployment declined, the rate of inflation usually accelerated. When total demand slackened and unemployment rose, the rate of inflation usually became more moderate. The chart highlights the fact that up until several years ago, the *sum* of each year's inflation rate and the preceding year's unemployment rate remained relatively stable,[2] although above the desired 6 per cent. This, in turn, implied that demand management policies could exert a significant influence on the rate of inflation.

---

[2]/See Note to Chart on page 12.

The Inflation-Unemployment Relationship, 1955-1972

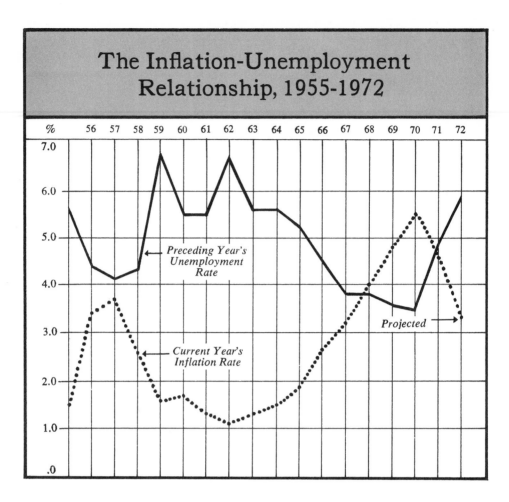

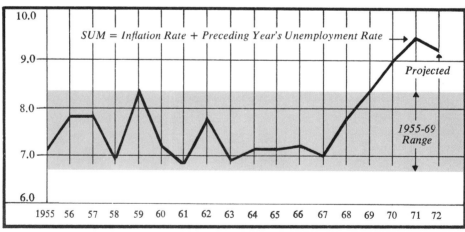

NOTE: The reason why the inflation-unemployment relationship can be expected to be more stable when each year's inflation rate is related to the unemployment rate for the preceding (rather than the current) year is that changes in demand conditions associated with given unemployment rates tend to affect prices only with some lag. The inverse relationship is still evident, however, when inflation and unemployment rates are compared for the same years.

Table One... | The Inflation-Unemployment Relationship, 1955-1972

IN PER CENT

Year	Inflation[1] Rate	Unemployment Rate	Previous Year's Unemployment Rate	Sum of Inflation Rate Plus Current Year's Unemployment Rate	Sum of Inflation Rate Plus Previous Year's Unemployment Rate
1955	1.5	4.4	5.6	5.9	**7.1**
1956	3.4	4.1	4.4	7.5	**7.8**
1957	3.7	4.3	4.1	8.0	**7.8**
1958	2.6	6.8	4.3	9.4	**6.9**
1959	1.6	5.5	6.8	7.1	**8.4**
1960	1.7	5.5	5.5	7.2	**7.2**
1961	1.3	6.7	5.5	8.0	**6.8**
1962	1.1	5.6	6.7	6.7	**7.8**
1963	1.3	5.6	5.6	6.9	**6.9**
1964	1.5	5.2	5.6	6.7	**7.1**
1965	1.9	4.5	5.2	6.4	**7.1**
1966	2.7	3.8	4.5	6.5	**7.2**
1967	3.2	3.8	3.8	7.0	**7.0**
1968	4.0	3.6	3.8	7.6	**7.8**
1969	4.8	3.5	3.6	8.3	**8.4**
1970	5.5	4.9	3.5	10.4	**9.0**
1971	4.6	5.9	4.9	10.5	**9.5**
1972	3.3[2]	—	5.9	—	**9.2[2]**

[1] Year-to-year change in GNP deflator
[2] Council of Economic Advisers projection
Source: Council of Economic Advisers, *Economic Report of the President, 1972.*

13.

During the past two or three years, however, this inverse relationship tended to break down. Although excessive demand disappeared toward the end of 1969 and unemployment started to rise significantly, the rate of price increase also continued to advance rapidly, reaching 5.5 per cent in 1970 and remaining close to that level in early 1971.[3] Thus the question arose as to whether entirely new influences were at work that required different or modified policy instruments.

These past shortcomings in economic performance do not necessarily indicate that the more traditional policy prescriptions (including many of those offered by this Committee) need to be changed. In fact, during some crucial periods these prescriptions have not been followed.* Nevertheless, the unsatisfactory stabilization record in recent years has led to extensive questioning of the adequacy of available policy tools:

- In the area of *general demand management,* the mid-1960's witnessed a major failure to make early and sufficient use of fiscal restraint in order to stem the excessive expansion of over-all demand associated mainly with the 1965 escalation of the Vietnam War. As a result, inflationary forces gained rapid momentum. This, in turn, placed unreasonable burdens on monetary policy and led to excessive swings in monetary conditions. A question remains, however, as to whether the failure to apply vigorous fiscal restraint merely reflected a unique set of historical circumstances or whether it manifested more intractable institutional difficulties inherent in our political system.

- When fiscal restraint finally was applied with considerable vigor, beginning in 1968, the desired dampening of aggregate demand was for a time substantially less pronounced than had been anticipated. In 1970-71, however, both the demand contraction and the rise in unemployment proved larger than expected.**

- In the area of *structural reforms,* past efforts to bring about significant improvements within a reasonable time span have proved disappointing. As a result, it does not seem likely that a quick

---

3/In the chart, this pronounced departure from earlier experience is highlighted by the fact that starting in 1969, the line depicting the sum of unemployment and inflation rates rises sharply above its earlier range. Of course, even with the same underlying economic structure, one should expect that the sum of these two variables would tend to be somewhat closer to the lower end of its normal range during the years of relatively high unemployment and somewhat closer to the upper end of the range in years of low unemployment. This consideration, however, does not alter the fact that the performance of the past two years has differed sharply from prior experience.

* See Memorandum by MR. JOHN D. HARPER, page 64.
** See Memorandum by MR. JOHN D. HARPER, page 65.

solution to the unemployment-inflation problem can be provided by supplementing appropriate aggregate demand policies with structural measures.

• In the light of the seemingly growing intractability of inflationary forces, furthermore, serious doubts had arisen by early 1971 as to whether the use of a more vigorous but essentially *voluntary incomes policy* to supplement demand management and structural policies would be sufficient to permit achievement of the stabilization objectives within a tolerable period of time. By mid-1971, there was a growing body of opinion that inflationary forces had gained such momentum that stronger medicine was required.*

As already noted, major questions remain as to whether past failures have reflected only temporary difficulties in implementing stabilization policies or whether they are indicative of more basic deficiencies in the available policy approaches. There are some who believe that most of the problem could have been resolved by a relatively brief shock treatment of severe deflation as a means of eliminating or sharply reducing inflationary expectations. Others see a need for the present compulsory control system and for making it more effective, but envisage a subsequent lifting of all compulsory restraints. Still others regard the underlying difficulties as substantially more deep-seated and believe that they can be overcome only through more basic changes in stabilization policy.

Finally, a view exists that there may be *no* set of feasible policies which can realistically be expected to result in the simultaneous achievement of reasonable price stability and high employment. According to this view, the public will inevitably have to become reconciled to a higher rate of inflation or a higher level of unemployment than has seemed acceptable up to now.

General Conclusions

We have carefully examined these questions and views in the light of the developments of recent years and of the initial experience with the New Economic Policy. The general conclusions that have emerged from this reappraisal are set forth below. A more detailed economic analysis and our specific policy recommendations are presented in the succeeding chapters.

---

* See Memorandum by MR. JOHN D. HARPER, page 65.

1. *We continue to believe that if the nation has the will,* the goal of steady economic growth at high levels of employment can and should be achieved without persistent inflation or chronic balance-of-payments deficits.* Indeed, control of inflation in our view remains an essential prerequisite for the attainment of the country's other economic objectives. We thus emphatically reject the advice of those who would have us give up the battle for simultaneous achievement of high employment and price stability even before a comprehensive effort has been mounted to win that battle.

While achievement of these objectives will take time, we do not feel that past or prospective difficulties in reaching them should cause policy makers to lower their sights. We continue to believe that the basic objective with respect to prices should be the attainment of price stability—not merely some reduction in the rate of inflation.[4] In the case of employment, the basic goal should be not merely to reduce the level of over-all unemployment to a given percentage of the labor force but to achieve a situation in which the number of job openings essentially matches the number of those seeking jobs at reasonable wages.[5]

2. *Sound management of total demand through appropriate fiscal and monetary policies must remain a central ingredient of any over-all national effort to achieve sustained high level prosperity without inflation.*** Our specific recommendations in this area, which are presented

---

[4]/This recommendation does not necessarily imply that we are aiming at zero growth in each of the major price indexes. As stated in *Fiscal and Monetary Policies for Steady Economic Growth* (January 1969), we identify absence of price inflation with "stability in the consumer price index after allowing for the inability of this index fully to reflect quality changes in goods and services produced." We recognize, moreover, that interim goals for the reduction of inflation under current governmental programs cannot realistically call for the complete elimination of inflationary tendencies within a very short period of time.

[5]/We recognize that until job vacancy and unemployment data are sufficiently improved so that progress toward this objective can be clearly calculated, the present measure of unemployment as a per cent of the labor force will have to be used in setting targets. See *Fiscal and Monetary Policies for Steady Economic Growth* (January 1969), p. 28. In assessing the significance of targets based on this measure, however, relevant changes in the structure of the labor market should be taken into account. Because the share of teenagers, young adults, and women in the labor force and total unemployment has markedly increased in recent years, for example, achievement of a 4 per cent "target" unemployment rate would apparently imply greater labor market tightness and stronger price pressures under today's conditions than under the conditions that existed ten or fifteen years ago. This emphatically does not mean that public concern with finding jobs for those seeking work should diminish; moreover, the labor market trends cited are at least in part expected to be reversed in coming years.

* See Memorandum by MR. MARVIN BOWER, page 65.
** See Memoranda by MR. JOHN D. HARPER, page 65, and by MR. FRANKLIN A. LINDSAY, page 66.

16.

in Chapter 3, reemphasize and build on the basic stabilization principles that CED has evolved over the years.

3. Improved management of total demand, however, is not enough to contain cost-push inflationary influences that arise from the supply side of the economy.* *A second key element in any successful effort to promote price stability must be a greatly intensified program to overcome basic structural obstacles to increased competition and productivity.* Such a program is considered in the last two chapters of this statement, in which we make recommendations for essential reforms in labor and product markets and discuss possible measures to reduce inflationary effects of governmental operations.**

4. *If the stabilization objectives are to be fully achieved, demand and structural measures will have to be supplemented for the foreseeable future with wage-price (or incomes) policies involving some direct governmental concern with significant wage and price decisions.**** In this connection, we urge that every effort be made to assure that the present compulsory wage-price control system will meet its targets.

5. We consider it essential that, at the same time, the basic aims of stabilization policies be kept in clear perspective. The goal is not only to achieve high employment with price stability, but to do so in an environment that provides the greatest feasible scope for competitive market forces. *The principal current task is not merely to make Phase II work but to do this in a way that will reduce the need for controls as rapidly as possible.* This means, in particular, that:

• While the temporary Phase II restraints are still in effect, vigorous and systematic efforts should be initiated to undertake needed structural reforms and to improve fiscal-monetary tools and their application. This will help to minimize the possibility that there will be long-continued and more widespread wage and price controls, which would be likely to lead to increasing distortions in the economy.

• A systematic procedure should be adopted that will create active incentives for moving as rapidly as feasible from the present compulsory control system toward increased reliance on free

---

* See Memorandum by MR. JOHN D. HARPER, page 66.
** See Memorandum by MR. JOHN D. HARPER, page 67.
*** See Memoranda by MR. JOHN D. HARPER, page 67, and by MR. HERMAN L. WEISS, page 67.

market mechanisms. A specific proposal is made in Chapter 4 for relating the pace of decontrol to the rate of reduction of the factors causing cost-push pressures.

Although we expect that use of the approach just outlined will in time eliminate most of the need for direct or indirect controls, *it is our view that some continuing direct governmental concern with wage and price decisions is desirable even over the longer run, and that statutory authority for compulsory controls should be continued on a standby basis.* The appropriate longer-run role of wage-price policies is discussed in Chapter 4.

In developing our recommendations for the types of improvements in general demand management policies, structural measures, and wage-price policies that deserve priority attention, we have been keenly aware that a successful approach to economic stabilization must take adequate account of the realities of the political process.[6] Clearly, the over-all strategy that should be pursued is not merely a matter of economics, but must find a reasonable chance of gaining acceptance by the Executive Branch, the Congress, and the public at large. At the same time, the fact must be faced that virtually all the important steps needed to move the economy toward noninflationary high employment are fraught with political difficulties. It would be unfortunate if excessive concern with short-term political feasibility should prevent vigorous action on the kinds of steps we are recommending.

---

[6]/Many of the issues involved were considered in earlier policy statements by this Committee. See, particularly, *Making Congress More Effective* (September 1970).

*See Memoranda by MR. MARVIN BOWER, by MR. JOHN D. HARPER, and by MR. HERMAN L. WEISS, pages 67 and 68.

2.

The Economic Setting for Future Policies

To DEVISE IMPROVED POLI-
CIES for reconciling high employment with price stability, policy makers must seek answers to at least two major questions. First, what accounts for the sharp deterioration of the inflation-unemployment relationship over the past few years? Second, what are the principal longer-term factors that made it so difficult to achieve a satisfactory combination of price movements and employment levels even prior to the recent experience? While fully definitive answers to these questions are not available, it is possible to identify enough of the key factors that have been at work to formulate a general policy approach to the price stability-high employment problem.

Deterioration of
the Inflation-Unemployment Relationship

There can be little doubt about the major reason for the severe upsurge of inflation in the mid-1960's. It lay in the sudden and excessive increase in total demand that accompanied the escalation of the Vietnam conflict and in the concomitant failure to contain this upsurge through timely and adequate fiscal-monetary restraint.

The fact that an excess of total demand over total supply results in inflation has long been known. What is much more difficult to explain is why the inflation persisted and, at times, even intensified long after aggregate demand had become deficient and the unemployment rate had moved to the 5-6 per cent range. In particular, these developments raise a basic question as to whether the strength of upward cost pressures should be regarded as temporary and can be counted on to disappear relatively soon—perhaps even without continued controls—or whether such pressures represent more intractable and possibly new and lasting structural changes in the economy.

According to one school of thought, the persistence of inflation in a period of relatively high unemployment can be attributed almost entirely to the delayed effects that the earlier excessive splurge of total demand has had on expectations. Undoubtedly, a cumulative spreading of inflationary psychology played a key role in the inflation of recent years. This was particularly true after the rate of price increase began to exceed 2 to 3 per cent per year. Therefore, measures to break that psychology must be an essential part of any successful effort to bring the inflationary spiral under control.

But as we explained more fully in our 1970 statement on *Further Weapons Against Inflation,*[1] it seems doubtful that the heightening of inflationary expectations *alone* can adequately explain the recent pronounced worsening in the inflation-unemployment relationship. Hence, it does not seem realistic to expect that the problem of inflation can be fully eliminated through measures to place a drastic dent in inflationary expectations by a temporary "shock treatment"—such as severe demand restraint or use of a compulsory wage-price freeze for a brief period.

A major reason for this is that extended periods of excessive demand do more than stimulate an inflationary spiral. They also create a variety of economic imbalances and distortions that can become independent generators of spiralling inflationary pressures. Because of rigidities and imperfections in the economy's response mechanisms, these pressures continue long after the excessive demand itself has disappeared and expectations have been modified. Such distortions tend to be particularly severe when the initial upsurge of demand produces an unusually rapid and unbalanced type of expansion, as was the case in 1965-68. An expansion of this kind subsequently causes those whose

---

[1] See *Further Weapons Against Inflation: Measures to Supplement General Fiscal and Monetary Policies* (November 1970), pp. 29-31.

relative earnings positions have worsened to make especially strenuous efforts to "catch up."

In the past few years, cumulative distortions in the "normal" pattern of wage differentials among industries served as a key element in the development of a cost-push spiral. During the period of substantial economic overheating and labor scarcities some groups of workers obtained exceptionally large wage gains. These gains tended to serve as a "bellwether" for the demands of other groups long after the original boom conditions had disappeared. Many of the larger unions had been locked into long-term contracts at the time the economy was overheated, and their contracts have come up for renegotiation only recently. There was pressure from these unions to bring their wages into a "normal" relationship with those granted earlier in contracts with other unions, which helped to perpetuate the high rate of increases that was originally geared to the prospect of continuing demand inflation. The very process of catching up, once started, has tended in turn to create new disparities in wage relationships, resulting in the emergence of a continuing "wage-wage spiral."

Our studies indicate that in 1968-70 the variations in wage increases were unusually large among manufacturing industries (the only sector for which reasonably reliable and comprehensive data on wage changes are available).[1] The variations diverged more sharply from what might be regarded as a stable pattern than at any time since 1957, when inflationary cost-push pressures were also gathering momentum. Hence, it was to be expected that there would also be strong pressures for the restoration of more traditional wage relationships through above-normal wage increases. Indeed, our studies suggest that this "wage-wage" mechanism, plus the changing age and sex composition of the labor force, account for a major share of the unusual recent divergence of the inflation-unemployment relationship from its longer-term pattern.

While these studies focused mainly on the manufacturing sector, it seems clear that a similar "spiral" mechanism also has been of significance for other sectors. Not only have "spillover" effects from wage increases in manufacturing industries been felt in other sectors but cost-push pressures originating outside the manufacturing sector have initiated spirals of their own.* The influence of "bellwether" effects has been

---

[1]The discussion in this and the following paragraph draws substantially on studies conducted by Arnold H. Packer and Seong Park of CED's research staff.

* See Memorandum by MR. HERMAN L. WEISS, page 68.

especially marked in the construction sector. Highly excessive wage increases for relatively small groups of construction workers have often tended to establish patterns for many other construction settlements. They also have served to influence wage demands by workers in some manufacturing and service industries.

In stressing the role of wages in the recent accelerated cost-push inflation, we do not mean to imply that all the blame should be attributed to labor. Even where wage increases were not immediately threatened, inflationary expectations appear to have made some firms unduly reluctant to forego price increases or institute price cuts when this became appropriate because of weakening markets.* In some cases, moreover, employers agreed to excessive wage demands and were willing and able to shift the burden of such settlements to the general public. This was done through higher prices, in the case of some private employers (for example, in construction); and through increased taxes or reductions in other types of expenditures, in the case of governmental bodies. Finally, the public itself has contributed to the cost-push spiral by its frequent failure to give adequate support to efforts designed to curtail this spiral.**

Whatever may have been the precise influences that helped to generate the cost-push inflation of the past few years, excessive wage increases had become a major generating element in this inflation by the time the New Economic Policy was instituted. Business pricing policies clearly had not resulted in an undue over-all rise in business profits. On the contrary, the share of business profits in national income had declined markedly from 1966 to 1970, even after allowances are made for the usual influence of a slowdown in economic activity; the effects of changed depreciation rules; and shifts from profit to interest as a payment to capital.

A number of important conclusions are suggested by this brief review of factors that contributed to the intensified cost inflation of the past few years:

First, it serves to reemphasize the central importance of sound fiscal and monetary policies for economic stabilization. Such policies not only put limits on the initial and direct inflationary effects of excessive over-all demand and unbalanced expansions but also avert the severe subsequent distortions that such excesses tend to induce in the cost-price structure.

---

* See Memorandum by MR. JOHN D. HARPER, page 68.
** See Memorandum by MR. HERMAN L. WEISS, page 69.

Second, it suggests that when such distortions become, or threaten to become, unusually pronounced, some direct government intervention in the process of wage and price determination may be essential if the distortions are to be diminished and a continuing spiral is to be avoided. This point had clearly been reached, or passed, by the time price and wage controls were initiated in August 1971.*

Third, it indicates that the need for active intervention in wage and price decisions may significantly diminish (though not necessarily disappear) once the degree of distortion has been substantially reduced with the help of such measures as wage and price controls.

Longer-Run Obstacles to Noninflationary High Employment

The factors described thus far go a long way toward explaining the sharp intensification of cost-push pressures in the recent past. However, they do not adequately account for the longer-run influences that have kept our economy from achieving truly noninflationary high employment.

What are these influences? Of key importance is the extent to which our economic system still has deeply imbedded restrictive institutions, practices, and attitudes that have grown up over many years primarily to provide protection against losses due to major recessions. These restrictions remain despite the fact that the country's commitment to the high employment objective has become increasingly firm and the risks of major recessions have been greatly reduced.

This has created a major asymmetry. On the one hand, there has been a lessening of inhibitions against excessive wage demands and price increases in the environment created by the national commitment to high employment—a commitment which in itself is highly desirable. The lessening of inhibitions seems to have become more pronounced in recent years with the growing awareness of underlying changes in the economic setting. On the other hand, the shift to the high employment commitment has not had its counterpart in a comparable reduction of downward rigidities in costs and prices. Of course, an important offset to inflationary pressures is provided by the greater productivity gains that tend to accrue when the economy experiences steady growth at high

---

*See Memorandum by MR. JOHN D. HARPER, page 69.

employment rather than frequent fluctuations. But to rectify the asymmetry more fully requires not only a significant strengthening of competitive market forces and incentives to promote increased productivity. It also requires far more vigorous steps to remove the many harmful rigidities in the system.

The nature of these longer-term structural impediments to price stability will be considered more fully in Chapters 5 and 6. They include various inflexibilities in the price structure. These can result from inappropriate business practices as well as from a wide range of governmental actions—for example, provision of wasteful subsidies and the use of unnecessary and inefficient regulations. Other impediments to price stability include numerous imperfections in the functioning of our labor markets as well as various deficiencies in existing labor-management statutes and the way they are administered.

The longer-run difficulties of reconciling high employment with price stability also have been affected by changes in the composition of the labor force. Compared with ten to fifteen years ago, a substantially smaller portion of the total labor force (and of total unemployment) currently consists of experienced males in the prime age groups. By the same token, there has been a marked increase in the relative share of teenagers, of other young adults, and of women of all ages, reflecting changes in labor force participation rates as well as in population patterns. As a result, the upward pressures on wages for given levels of over-all unemployment have tended to increase. This is because experienced males of prime working age often have the greatest influence on union wage bargaining and because the relative shortage of men in these age brackets tends to add to their bargaining power. Over the next decade, however, the share of 25- to 35-year-old men in the labor force is expected to increase by as much as one-third. At the same time, the labor force as a whole is expected to expand at a markedly faster pace than in the 1960's. Such developments ought to have some dampening effects on future wage demands. Nevertheless, labor union pressures can be expected to remain substantial. This may result, in particular, from greater militancy of the generation of workers that is moving into the prime age groups—a militancy that partly reflects the current tendencies toward questioning of established authority, but that can also be traced to changes in union structure brought about by earlier legislation.

Another obstacle to a reduction of longer-term inflationary forces has been the growing relative importance of the service and governmental

Table Two | Distribution of Employment and Output by Industry

(Per cent)

	EMPLOYMENT[1] Per cent Distribution				OUTPUT[2] Per cent Distribution			
	1950	1960	1970	Average Annual Rate of Change 1950-70	1950	1960	1970	Average Annual Rate of Change 1950-70
ALL INDUSTRIES	100.0	100.0	100.0	1.9	100.0	100.0	100.0	3.6
Agriculture	5.0	3.4	1.9	−2.8	5.7	4.7	3.5	1.1
Construction	4.9	5.0	4.9	1.9	4.6	4.4	3.2	1.8
Manufacturing and Mining	33.0	30.6	28.0	1.1	32.7	31.6	32.5	3.6
Manufacturing	31.1	29.4	27.1	1.2	29.7	28.9	30.2	3.7
SERVICES	42.1	42.8	45.0	2.3	46.5	48.8	51.4	4.1
Transportation, Communications, Public Utilities	8.0	6.5	5.9	0.4	8.6	9.2	10.7	4.7
Trade, Finance, Services	34.1	36.1	39.1	2.6	37.9	39.6	40.7	4.0
GOVERNMENT	15.1	18.2	20.1	3.4	10.1	9.6	9.7	3.4
Federal	7.5	8.5	8.2	2.4		(Not available)		
State and Local	7.6	9.7	11.9	4.2				

[1]/Number of full-time equivalent employees. [2]/Gross product in constant (1958) dollars

Source: U.S. Department of Commerce: Bureau of Economic Analysis, *Survey of Current Business*, tables 6.4 and 1.21

sectors, as shown in Table Two. From 1950 to 1970, over 80 per cent of the net increase in national employment was attributable to these sectors. As a result, their percentage share in total employment rose significantly while that of manufacturing and mining declined.[2]

Productivity gains in many services and in government (at least as now measured) have usually been significantly lower on the average than in the goods-producing sectors. These developments have tended to add to the difficulties of maintaining given over-all rates of productivity gain and of averting upward price pressures. For the future, they clearly suggest that major emphasis should be placed on efforts to raise productivity in the service and government sectors.

The preceding discussion has been concerned primarily with the sources of inflationary bias. However, many of the influences cited help to explain why it has proved so difficult to reduce total unemployment at given levels of inflation. In a properly functioning market economy, the supply of labor should continuously adapt itself to the demands for labor; and with major shifts in the composition of labor supply, various adaptations in the demand for labor are also desirable. But in our economy, these adaptations are all too frequently prevented by (1) restrictive union and business practices that affect entry into occupations, particularly because of race, sex, and age discrimination; and (2) governmental restrictions such as minimum wage laws that discourage adaptations in the demand for labor by failing to differentiate between prime age workers and teenage, older, and handicapped workers.

For some groups in the labor force—particularly for blacks, women, and young people—these restrictions have led to much higher than average unemployment and much greater difficulties in obtaining adequate on-the-job training. Serious technical deficiencies in the ways in which our labor markets function have further added to the problem of matching job seekers and job vacancies. These tendencies—by contributing to a less efficient utilization of the country's total labor force and holding down potential productivity gains—have both magnified the unemployment problem and added another inflationary element.

It is likely that all of the structural influences cited above have contributed to the economy's apparent long-term inflationary bias, although no reliable means exist for assessing the quantitative importance of each factor. It seems clear, however, that an effective long-term pro-

---

[2] In terms of output, however, the relative share of the goods-producing sector vis-a-vis services and government has declined only very slightly since 1950.

26.

gram to achieve noninflationary high employment will have to place major reliance on efforts to overcome such structural barriers and to produce more flexible and competitive product and labor markets.

In some instances, of course, the removal of existing structural impediments will produce only a one-time improvement in price performance. But this by no means will always be the case. In fact, failure to deal actively with the elimination of harmful rigidities could well contribute to continuing inflation. For it would serve as an increasingly serious barrier to the economy's effective adaptation to numerous fundamental changes—including the rapid advances in technology; the changing composition of the labor force; the shifting character of final demands; and the changing U.S. position in world markets.

Even with very energetic efforts to achieve structural reforms, however, the task of overcoming many of the basic sources of inflationary bias in the economy described in this chapter is bound to be difficult and long-extended. It is this consideration which leads to the conclusion that some continuing governmental capability to use wage-price restraints as a supplementary tool is likely to be needed for the foreseeable future to assure adequate progress toward attainment of noninflationary high employment.

3.

Fiscal and Monetary Measures

WE HAVE STRESSED that appropriate management of total demand remains an essential prerequisite for any effective program of economic stabilization. But in the light of the experience of recent years, can the traditional instruments of fiscal and monetary policy still be considered adequate to perform this task?

By and large, the record shows that when the traditional instruments were used promptly and vigorously, they had very substantial and relatively predictable economic effects. It is true that there were far too many occasions in recent years when aggregate demand deviated sharply from what would have been desirable and from the standards that we had recommended. But for the most part, this did not result from an inherent ineffectiveness of the available policy instruments. Rather, it reflected a failure to apply these instruments vigorously once action became appropriate in the light of reasonable policy guides—a failure that was most conspicuous in the mid-1960's, when strong fiscal restraint was clearly called for. Some questions remain as to why the subsequent imposition of the income tax surcharge in 1968 did not dampen excessive demand as quickly as many expected. However, it now appears that much of the lag can be attributed to the fact that the momentum of the long-continued inflation had become greater than widely realized and that mistakes in forecasts resulted in a premature easing of monetary policy.[1]

Of course, it may well be that some longer-run changes have been under way in the response pattern of our economy to fiscal and monetary influences, and that this strengthens the case for the development of some additional policy instruments to influence demand. For example, it might be desirable to give an increased role in stabilization policy to variable consumption taxes. Our Subcommittee on Revenue Needs and the Tax System is currently examining these matters in more detail. We recognize, too, that the obstacles to fully effective application of demand management tools often reflect even more basic factors. In particular, the public's demands for improved governmental services have all too frequently risen far more than its willingness to pay for these services. In part, of course, this resistance has reflected widespread doubts that expenditure increases would be put to fully effective use—doubts that need to be overcome by energetic governmental actions to improve productivity and achieve better control of costs. But beyond this, intensive efforts are needed to foster a better public understanding of the fact that payment for necessary services basically cannot be avoided and that the key future issue is likely to be whether the payment will be made either by higher taxes or relative cutbacks in other services, or whether it is to be exacted through inflation. There has also been a frequent lack of political will to make timely and adequate use of demand management tools when they are needed.

We believe, therefore, that more effective stabilization of total demand calls primarily for greater political willingness to make prompt and appropriate use of the existing policy instruments. This willingness can be strengthened by better public understanding of the policy rules which are appropriate and by increased flexibility in the use of the policy instruments available.

---

[1]The sharp monetary and credit tightening of 1966 exerted a pronounced restraining influence on overall demand, even though its severely discriminatory impact on the housing and local government sectors made it a far less desirable form of restraint than a more even-handed combination of fiscal and monetary measures would have produced. And while the demand restraints imposed during and subsequent to 1968 did not take hold as quickly as first anticipated, they clearly played the key role in inducing a slow-down of economic growth for several years.

The Development of CED's Stabilizing Budget Policy

As long as a quarter of a century ago, this Committee developed the basic guide for setting federal tax rates and expenditures that has become known as "CED's" stabilizing budget policy. As usually defined, the policy calls for the setting of tax rates and expenditure programs to yield a moderate surplus in the federal budget when the economy is operating at high employment and reasonably stable prices. The policy relies for its effectiveness on the fact that when the economy fluctuates the actual relation between revenues and expenditures tends to vary automatically in a stabilizing direction, becoming more expansive when the economy is depressed and more restrictive when the economy is booming or inflationary. It was initially felt that these so-called automatic or "built-in" stabilizers in the budget could be counted upon to rectify a large share of any likely deviations from a steady course of the economy at high employment. As a result, it was assumed that the remaining economic stabilization task could be entrusted mainly to a flexible monetary policy, and that discretionary fiscal actions would then be needed only in very exceptional cases.

This approach had two major advantages over the more traditional rules of budget-making and particularly over efforts to seek an annual balance in the actual budget under all circumstances. First, it distinguished between the budget's effects on the economy and the economy's effect on the budget. Thus, it made clear that deficits in the actual budget at a time of economic weakness (or relatively large surpluses at times of excessive aggregate demand) may not be merely tolerable but may be required to restore sound economic conditions. Second, the rule that the budget should be aimed at achieving a moderate surplus at high employment provided a needed source of long-term budgetary discipline. It meant that current expenditure and tax decisions had to be made against the perspective of their longer-term effects on the desirable division of national resources between the public and private sectors.

Our Committee has continued to adhere to the fundamental precepts underlying the stabilizing budget rules. Over the years, however, we have modified our more specific formulation of these rules in a number of respects. This was particularly true of our 1969 policy statement, *Fiscal and Monetary Policies for Steady Economic Growth,* which included a major reassessment of CED's fiscal and monetary policy positions. One of the conclusions reached was that the built-in stabilizers in the fiscal system may often be inadequate by themselves to bring about the desired economic objectives. As a result, there may be need for additional discretionary actions that will affect both tax rates and expenditures at fairly frequent intervals. In the light of this finding, we recommended (1) that the level of taxes and expenditures as well as the balance in the federal budget ought to be reviewed on an annual basis, and (2) that discretionary changes in tax rates and in some expenditures should be made whenever such a review suggested this was appropriate. Moreover, we took the position that it was essential that the required fiscal changes could be made promptly and flexibly. To achieve this goal, we recommended that the President be granted discretion by the Congress to raise or lower income tax payments by up to 10 per cent, in a form to be decided by the Congress and subject to Congressional veto.

Over the past decade, the principles embodied in our budget rules have gained increasing acceptance by the federal government, even though actual policy has deviated substantially from these principles on numerous occasions. During the Kennedy-Johnson Administration, the concept of a full employment budget was highlighted in the President's Economic Reports. Moreover, the concept was used effectively to explain the logic of relying on tax cuts to stimulate the economy at a time of lagging economic growth and budget deficits. The present Administration has gone even further. It has formally incorporated the high employment budget concept in its official budget documents, beginning with the fiscal 1972 budget, and geared its over-all fiscal policy to the attainment of balance in the high employment budget.*

Reassessing the High Employment Budget Rules

We welcome the increased emphasis on high employment budget principles in fiscal policy formulation. Nevertheless, we are concerned by the risk that these principles may be used in too mechanical a manner and that the underlying logic for using them may not always be sufficiently kept in mind in public discussion. While pursuit of these principles is of key importance as a starting point for a sound fiscal policy, it does not exhaust the steps needed for responsible fiscal management.

*See Memorandum by MR. MARVIN BOWER, page 69.

Fiscal policy makers always face a possible conflict between the needs of short-term economic stabilization and appropriate longer-term national resource allocation. Reliance on a rule that gears current policy to a budget balance or surplus at high employment can probably serve to resolve that conflict in a majority of circumstances, particularly when the high employment budget is properly defined. However, situations also arise with some frequency in which the amount of fiscal stimulus or restraint needed by the economy over the short run is quite inappropriate for the longer run. The public should understand clearly that in such cases it makes no sense to interpret the rule for balance in the high employment budget so strictly that it prevents the economy from moving toward high employment in the first place. Moreover, even if the high employment budget is in balance, it cannot be assumed automatically that current fiscal actions carry no future inflationary risks.

The essential consideration is that special precautions need to be taken whenever there are deviations from the basic rule for maintaining a surplus or balance in the high employment budget. This is equally true when other signs of future fiscal difficulties appear. In such cases, policy makers should be placed under an extra obligation—and given the means —to assure that the additional near-term stimulus or restraint will not subsequently lead to a substantial overshooting of the mark but can be promptly reversed when required.

We are concerned that in this respect adequate preparations have not been made. Indeed, current trends suggest that potential inflationary pressures on the budget a few years hence will reach alarming proportions unless better advance preparations are made to avert such an outcome. To handle this problem, we urge that, in conjunction with basic reliance on the stabilizing high employment budget rules, the following approaches receive special emphasis in fiscal policy making.

First, we recommend that when the economic situation calls for added fiscal stimulus, every effort should be made to give preference to measures that contain a built-in feature for phasing out the stimulus when high employment is reached, rather than to measures that will produce continuing or even growing future budgetary drains. Examples of self-limiting expenditures with "formula flexibility"[2] are the extended unemployment compensation payments and outlays for temporary public

---

[2]/With a requirement of balance or surplus in the high employment budget, there is an automatic incentive for the use of such measures to the extent they are excluded in calculating this balance, as was done in the fiscal 1973 budget.

service employment which have recently been enacted. These are geared by law to the national unemployment level and must be phased out as high employment is reached.

Second, explicit contingency plans should be developed *now* for dealing with the risks of excess claims on fiscal resources at high employment that are embodied in current and prospective tax and spending programs. In this connection, special attention should be focused on the extent to which expenditure and tax incentive programs that now involve only small costs can lead to sharply burgeoning costs in later years. While the latest budget document included useful estimates of the potential "fiscal margin" in 1976, future analyses of the five-year fiscal outlook should be presented in substantially greater detail. These analyses should show a year-by-year and program-by-program breakdown and also provide the public with a clearer view of major policy alternatives.[3]

We also recommend that the federal government propose within the relatively near future—and not later than in early 1973—the broad types of measures that ought to be taken to assure that a budgetary surplus or at least balance can be achieved when high employment is actually reached. Even though the immediate policy focus must still be on adequate expansion, the long-term problems of rational over-all resource allocation and of obtaining adequate revenues are urgent—requiring very hard choices that involve tax increases or some major expenditure cuts, or both. Unless the groundwork for such choices is laid several years ahead of time, the chances are dim that they can be effectively implemented when the need arises.[4]

Third, we believe that even if such longer term fiscal contingency plans are instituted, a major need remains for developing additional means of fiscal flexibility. **In particular, we feel that given the strong expansionary thrust of fiscal policy, there is now a greater need than ever to implement this Committee's 1969 recommendation that the President be given discretionary authority to raise or lower income taxes by limited amounts, subject to Congressional veto.*** We are less concerned with the precise method by which this flexibility might be achieved

---

[3]/See our recommendations in *Improving Federal Program Performance* (September 1971), pp. 53-55.

[4]/The Subcommittee of the Research and Policy Committee on Revenue Needs and the Tax System is giving detailed consideration to the longer-range issues of fiscal priorities.

*See Memorandum by MR. ALEXANDER L. STOTT, page 69.

33.

than with seeing that a procedure of this kind is instituted well before a new crisis makes the need painfully evident to all.

We also repeat our earlier recommendation that all federal programs and activities be automatically subject to searching Congressional review at regular intervals, generally a maximum of four years and established on a rotational schedule.[5] Such reviews should be applied to all programs that imply drains on the budget, including not only ordinary expenditures and federal grants-in-aid but also all credit subsidies and tax incentives.

The thrust of our recommendations in this section is simple. The longer-term requirements of fiscal discipline must not be allowed to inhibit the provision of the budgetary stimulus needed for adequate economic recovery. But if policy makers are to push hard on the accelerator, they must also have full assurance that they will be able to put on the brakes promptly and vigorously when this is required.

Federal Credit and Guarantee Programs. We believe that the stabilizing budget rule should relate to the high employment budget on a National Income Accounts (NIA) basis. This provides a better measure of *fiscal* effects than the unified budget. The latter includes a number of lending programs which have their main effects on credit markets and tend to be affected by monetary and debt management policy rather than fiscal policy.[6] However, as a complement to the high employment budget on the National Income Accounts basis there is need for more integrated measurement and assessment of the pressures which federal and federally-assisted loan and guarantee programs exert on financial markets and on the over-all allocation of credit resources. The programs that need to be covered go far beyond those still included in the unified budget. In part, this is because of the pronounced recent trend to move credit programs out of the budget by shifting from "direct" to "indirect" lending techniques.

An integrated process for reviewing the effects of these federal and federally-assisted credit and guarantee programs, however, should merely be part of a needed effort to (1) bring the administration of these programs under better over-all control and (2) see that they are more adequately coordinated with monetary, fiscal, and debt manage-

---

[5] See *Making Congress More Effective* (September 1970), p. 32.

[6] It should be noted that, on an NIA basis, a moderate high employment budget *surplus* may often be equivalent to a high employment budget balance on a unified basis, though this need not always be the case.

34.

ment policy. **As a useful step in this direction, we endorse the proposed establishment of a Federal Financing Bank to coordinate federal agency borrowing and guarantee programs.** In our view, however, even stronger means must be found to exert effective over-all control of the pro-liferating federal activities in the credit markets. **We recommend, therefore, that the President be authorized to place limits on the total volume of loan guarantees and of borrowing by federal and federally-sponsored credit agencies.**[7] These limitations should be subject to Congressional review and should extend to all government-sponsored credit agencies (including those that are privately owned) which benefit from either an actual or an implied federal guarantee of their securities.

Monetary Policy, Selective Credit and Tax Programs, and the Over-all Policy Mix. The excessive burden that has been placed on monetary policy in recent years should be reduced, making it easier to avoid undesirably wide swings in credit conditions. This should be possible with improved fiscal policies and better coordination of federal credit programs, and given the prospects for increased flexibility in international adjustment mechanisms. Monetary policy, however, should continue to serve as a flexible instrument of economic stabilization.

We believe that adoption of the recommendations made in this chapter would greatly reduce any possible future need for resorting to selective measures when general monetary policy is tightened. In line with the position taken in our 1970 policy statement on *Further Weapons Against Inflation,* we do not rule out the possibility that under certain circumstances some selective credit controls may have to play a role in the over-all stabilization effort, at least as a means of reducing the unevenness of the impact of general monetary restraint.*

In the past, a highly disproportionate share of the burden of tight monetary policy has tended to fall on housing. Uneven effects of such tightness have also been felt by states and localities and by smaller business firms. This is not only inequitable but has often tended to impose a special penalty on activities of relatively high social priority. The resultant instability of output and employment in the construction industry, moreover, has often added to inflationary cost pressures by undermining productivity, encouraging restrictive practices, and impeding orderly long-range planning.

---

[7]/Specific means of carrying out this recommendation are being studied by our Sub-committee on Financing the Nation's Housing Needs.

*See Memorandum by MR. ALLAN SPROUL, page 69.

Such effects can in part be alleviated by special measures to assist the mortgage and municipal markets and by basic improvements in the functioning of these markets. Under certain conditions, however, the discriminatory effects of general monetary restraint on housing and the state and local sector can probably be averted only if selective measures are used that impinge directly on other sectors—notably on business investment. It is in this context that credit controls may prove useful.*

A possible alternative would be to rely on selective fiscal devices, such as a variable investment tax credit,** an approach which has recently been endorsed by the Federal Reserve Board. The analysis underlying the Board's recommendation devoted major attention to the potential drawbacks of possible selective credit control devices. However, it did not concern itself as fully with the considerable drawbacks that frequent changes in the investment tax credit could entail. Further intensive studies should be carried out to determine the relative roles that future stabilization policies might assign to selective credit and tax measures. Detailed consideration is being given to this issue by our Subcommittees on Revenue Needs and the Tax System and on Financing the Nation's Housing Needs.***

While monetary policy has tended to have especially pronounced sectoral effects, it is important to keep in mind that when policy makers choose particular stabilization policy instruments or a stabilization "policy-mix," they also are invariably making choices about resource allocation. For example, excise tax changes generally have their principal effects on consumer durables; changes in income tax exemptions tend to affect consumer spending generally; the investment tax credit influences business investment; and government expenditure changes affect particular types of public or private activities. We believe that in the future design of over-all stabilization strategies, more intensive and systematic attention should be devoted to the impact which the choice of stabilization instruments exerts on the desirable allocation of resources in terms of national goals.

---

*See Memorandum by MR. ALEXANDER L. STOTT, page 70.
**See Memorandum by MR. ALEXANDER L. STOTT, page 70.
***See Memorandum by MR. HERMAN L. WEISS, page 70.

4.

The Role of Wage-Price Policies

IMPLEMENTATION of the preceding recommendations for improving the design and application of fiscal and monetary policies should go a long way toward enabling the nation to meet its stabilization objectives. But, in view of the various structural and cost-push influences described in Chapter 2, it does not appear likely that improved management of over-all demand will be sufficient by itself to reconcile high employment and price stability.*

As indicated earlier, the principal means of dealing with these elements of inflationary bias in our economy should consist of basic structural reforms that will remove rigidities in our labor and product markets and strengthen the forces of competition. A priority program for such structural reforms is set forth in the next two chapters. It is clear, however, that achievement of such reforms is often a formidable task and will in many cases take considerable time. In the interim, it appears that it will also be necessary to apply policy measures other than those proposed in the fiscal and monetary areas if the conflict between high employment and price stability is to be resolved soon, and avoided in the future. The principal additional policy instrument available for this purpose is wage-price policies.

*See Memorandum by MR. JOHN D. HARPER, page 70.

Wage-Price Policies:
An Overview

Because of the structural rigidities now present in our economy, we believe that some continuing direct governmental concern with significant wage and price decisions must play a role in the over-all stabilization strategy. This role, however, must be clearly supplementary to reliance on appropriate fiscal-monetary policies and basic structural reforms, and needs to be explicitly identified as such to the public.

In our 1970 statement, *Further Weapons Against Inflation,* we indicated that a forceful policy of voluntary wage-price restraints was appropriate under the circumstances then existing. For the reasons outlined earlier, we recognize that in 1971 a strong case existed for the application of compulsory controls. To the extent that they succeed in dampening inflationary expectations, and in reducing the distortions brought on by the earlier excessive demand inflation, these controls should be able to make an important contribution to the over-all stabilization effort.*

But what should be the duration of the present mandatory controls? And what role, if any, should wage-price policies of any kind play over the longer run? Our answers to these questions can be summarized as follows:

1. The compulsory control features of Phase II should be maintained until—but only until—the program shows reasonable success in meeting its targets.[1] To drop it prematurely might merely create subsequent pressures for the imposition of even more burdensome controls. On the other hand, maintaining the program too long would make a reasonably smooth return to freer markets increasingly difficult.

2. Over the longer run there is need to maintain, at least on a standby basis, some orderly mechanism to protect the public interest in containing inflation that results from important wage and price decisions. This mechanism should rely essentially on voluntary cooperation and on its role in educating the public to the realities of the forces at work, although statutory standby

---

[1]/Official statements have placed these targets at a 2-3 per cent rate of price increase and a drop in the unemployment rate to "the neighborhood of 5 per cent" by the end of 1972.

*See Memorandum by MR. JOHN D. HARPER, page 71.

authority for compulsory controls should be continued as long as necessary.*

3. The critically important consideration, however, is to make certain that the over-all stabilization strategy puts the principal types of policy tools in proper perspective. **The basic aim of policy makers should be to achieve their stabilization goals by primary reliance on fiscal and monetary policies as well as structural reforms. They should move away from direct or indirect controls of wages and prices as quickly as is feasible within the constraints mentioned earlier.** As many incentives as possible should be built into the existing control system to relate the pace of decontrol directly to the speed with which cost-push pressures in various segments of the economy diminish or disappear.

Speeding Up Decontrol: A Proposal. More specifically, we believe there is need for an explicit procedure that will permit selective removal of compulsory controls when there is evidence that the industries or firms involved have met specified criteria. **We recommend that the Cost of Living Council develop and publicly announce the general types of criteria that will be used to govern decontrol decisions.**

It is encouraging that the Cost of Living Council has recognized that, in general, mandatory controls are not likely to be needed in areas of the economy where competitive forces are strong and price competition is active. The exemption of a large number of the smaller retail trade establishments was appropriate under this criterion, and should relieve the program of a very large and unnecessary administrative burden.**

Additional criteria that could qualify industries or firms for decontrol should also be spelled out, however. Particularly important among these are criteria relating to demonstrated progress within an industry in overcoming structural impediments to competitive cost and price performance. Others would relate to the behavior of profits as well as to the actual record of cost-price performance.*** Thus, decontrol might become appropriate if an industry's wage and price performance had been better than the legally required norm by some specified margin and for a given period of months. Another criterion would relate

---

*See Memoranda by MR. JOHN D. HARPER, and by MR. HERMAN L. WEISS, page 71.
**See Memorandum by MR. HERMAN L. WEISS, page 71.
***See Memorandum by MR. HERMAN L. WEISS, page 71.

to known indicators of potential future stability or instability in the industry—for example, the stage of the wage negotiation process and the extent to which demands for "catch-ups" remain a problem. Finally, partial or full exemption from the general compulsory mechanism might be granted in cases where special organizational arrangements are worked out to cope with the inflationary problems of particular sectors or industries. Such arrangements are already being used in the construction industry and are being introduced in the medical care sector.*

The initiative with respect to decontrol should not be left solely in the hands of the administrators of the stabilization program. This is why we believe that an additional procedure is needed for triggering reviews that could lead to reduction or termination of compulsory restraints. **Specifically, we recommend that business, labor, and other affected groups in particular economic sectors be permitted (either separately or jointly) to petition the Cost of Living Council for full or partial exemption from the existing Phase II control mechanism on the basis of evidence that the announced criteria for decontrol have been met.**

The petition procedure could be an especially useful device for building vitally needed incentives for moving from the Phase II system toward decontrol, thereby combatting the natural tendency of all control agencies to hold onto their powers. Under the petition procedure, the control agencies would have to assume the burden of proof for showing why particular activities that meet specified criteria should not be exempt from the controls. At the same time, the petition procedure would provide a positive incentive for all those affected to create the conditions that would make controls no longer necessary.

The kind of selective reductions of compulsory controls we suggest by no means rule out a tightening of some elements of the program in the near term future to the extent that this is needed to reach the stabilization goals.** Nor would it preclude an across-the-board lifting of the controls once this appeared justified in the light of national economic performance. The important thing is to begin the process of disengagement from compulsory controls at the earliest appropriate stage, and to do it in a way that best facilitates the transition to a viable longer-term stabilization strategy.

*See Memorandum by MR. JOHN D. HARPER, page 72.
**See Memorandum by MR. JOHN D. HARPER, page 72.

Wage-Price Policies Over the Longer Run. How active a part should wage-price policies play in such a longer-term strategy? As already indicated, we believe that statutory standby authority for compulsory controls should be continued. After the present price and employment goals have been reached, however, direct compulsory controls would no longer be needed except, perhaps, in a few sectors in which cost-push pressures are especially virulent—for example, construction. The government should, nevertheless, call on all sectors of the economy to cooperate with a voluntary policy of wage and price restraint that is geared to the broad over-all stabilization objectives. **A Presidentially-appointed board should promulgate general guidelines for responsible wage and price behavior in both the private and public sectors and broadly monitor the extent to which actual behavior in different economic sectors and industries conforms to these guidelines.** *

Some of the administrative mechanisms that have been developed in connection with Phase II might be used to carry out these functions. However, the precise nature of the organizational apparatus for a longer-term price-incomes policy should only be determined after there has been more experience with the existing mechanisms. It seems quite likely that an effective and durable longer-term arrangement would call for replacement of the present apparatus with a single board concerned with both incomes and prices. Such a board should be entirely composed of individuals who represent the general public, but be assisted by an advisory board on which the major interest groups would be represented.

The board would be authorized to make periodic reports on the extent to which inflationary forces were being brought under control, although it would avoid *ad hoc* interference with particular wage-price decisions. If evidence accumulated that the cost-price behavior in particular industries or sectors deviated significantly from the broad guidelines, the board would be expected to undertake special reviews of such situations and call the conclusions to public attention. In addition, the President would have authority to refer relevant cases to the board for study.

To the extent possible, the board should search for solutions that would avoid renewed recourse to direct controls. Thus, it might develop recommendations for coping with inflationary pressures in particular

---

*See Memorandum by MR. JOHN D. HARPER, page 72.

industries through cooperative efforts to raise productivity. Should it find that the problem stemmed largely from unjustifiable deviations from the standards it had set forth, it could first ask the parties involved for voluntary compliance with the guidelines. If this proved unsuccessful, it could recommend that the government reimpose compulsory controls for the industry concerned.

Such a reimposition of controls would not be permitted on an *ad hoc* basis but should occur only in accordance with the "due process" procedure just outlined. The business and labor groups in the industry involved would have to be given an opportunity to present their views at a hearing if they so desired. None of the parties involved would be subject to legal penalties unless they had first been explicitly enjoined from taking specified actions and had then refused to comply. This feature of the program would need to be made very explicit to relieve both management and labor of fears that the "voluntary" system would leave them subject to arbitrary or capricious treatment.

Nature of the Longer-Term Guidelines. The longer-term standards for wage and price behavior that the board might promulgate would in many respects be quite similar to those developed in connection with Phase II. There would be some important differences, however.

First, only relatively broad norms for wage and price behavior would be set forth—not a large network of detailed regulations. Such norms should not merely relate to allowable wage and price changes in individual years, but should also place limits on increases that might be granted under escalator clauses in long-term contracts.

Second, the national target for desirable price behavior should gradually be reduced from the current goal—i.e., holding the annual rate of price increase to 2½ per cent—to target values that come successively closer to the long-term objective of price stability.*

Third, the longer-term guidelines should place greater stress on the need for transmitting part of the benefits of productivity gains to the consumer in the form of price reductions.

Fourth, greater flexibility should be permitted with respect to allowable wage rate and profit rate increases in order to strengthen productivity and investment incentives. There should be more active scope for bargaining over the relative income shares of labor and capital so long as this does not cause the price guidelines to be exceeded.

---

*See Memorandum by MR. JOHN R. COLEMAN, page 72.

As discussed in Chapter 5, for example, labor might more frequently be permitted to obtain wage increases in excess of the basic norm if this can be justified on the basis of productivity gains directly attributable to special labor efforts in particular firms—such as agreement to terminate various restrictive union practices—and if there is adherence to the other longer-term standards just outlined. Wage increases in excess of the general guideline that are based on such "productivity bargains" should remain in effect for a limited period only, though they might be spread over several years. Other exceptions from the guidelines could continue to be required for low-paid or intermittently-employed workers; for attracting people into areas and occupations of extreme labor shortage; and for some other carefully defined situations.

As regards profits, we welcome the fact that under the existing Phase II programs, direct control of total profits has been explicitly rejected as a stabilization tool. Use of such a technique is not only unnecessary if the wage and price control mechanism works properly, but would seriously undermine the incentives needed in a soundly functioning competitive system. Rejection of efforts to impose direct restraints on the volume of profits should continue to be a basic policy principle under any longer-run wage-price policy. At the same time, there would need to be clearer recognition of the fact that under some circumstances an expansion in profit *margins,* as well as in total profits, is not only compatible with over-all price stability but a necessary condition for moving toward that goal. To a significant extent, productivity gains depend on increased investment in new plant and equipment. Unless profit rates are adequate in relation to invested capital, the needed additional investment will not be forthcoming.*

---

*See Memoranda by MR. JOSEPH L. BLOCK, and by MR. HERMAN L. WEISS, pages 72 and 73.

5.

Structural Reforms: The Private Sector

A WIDE RANGE of basic structural reforms is urgently needed if the economy is to have genuinely noninflationary high employment.

In the past, this Committee has made numerous recommendations for such structural improvements, particularly in our 1970 policy statement, *Further Weapons Against Inflation*. We shall not attempt to repeat all of these recommendations here. Rather, we highlight in this and the following chapter the approaches to structural improvements that, in our view, would make particularly significant contributions to reducing the need for long-term controls and thus deserve priority attention.*

Improving Productivity and Orderly Adjustment to Change

The major stress in any program of structural reform should be on strengthening competitive forces and incentives, fostering greater flexibility and adaptability to change, and increasing productivity. Such a positive emphasis offers the best chance of securing acceptance of the needed changes and of helping to create a basic environment of healthy economic growth and high employment.

---

* See Memorandum by MR. DAVIDSON SOMMERS, page 73.

44.

It is clear that much more intensive efforts to foster productivity gains are needed. We welcome the fact that by statute the National Commission on Productivity has now been given substantially increased responsibilities and received authorization for a sizable full-time staff. It is also encouraging that the statute calls for the creation of regional and local productivity councils. **We urge that the National Commission on Productivity make the fullest use of this new authority and that adequate funding be provided for its activities as proposed by the Administration. We also favor strong emphasis in federal programs on assistance to research and development and welcome the provision of more adequate incentives for productive capital investment, such as the investment tax credit.**

As already noted, it is in the service sector, including government, that both the need and the opportunities for increasing productivity appear to be especially great.* For many types of services, significant productivity improvements should be feasible through (1) substantially increased reliance on mechanization and computerization; and (2) more modern and effective management approaches, such as the increased "accountability" requirements in education recommended in our policy statement, *Education for the Urban Disadvantaged.*[1] It should be possible to achieve other important productivity gains in the service sector by more energetic efforts to widen the size of existing markets in order to obtain more economies of scale; by more rational manpower utilization; and by the development of more efficient distribution and delivery systems. Productivity improvements in the governmental sector are discussed in Chapter 6.

A related effort of major importance should be devoted to wide-ranging improvements in the functioning of labor markets. These should be designed to produce a much more efficient matching of labor demand and supply and to bring about a much fuller utilization of the potentials of our human resources. Paradoxical as it may seem, our labor markets are frequently characterized by the coexistence of serious shortages for some types of labor with persistent unemployment for many other groups of workers. Part of the answer to this problem must lie in the development of innovative, broader and more effective programs to upgrade the training and education of the disadvantaged and

---

[1]/See *Education for the Urban Disadvantaged* (March 1971), pp. 59-66.
*See Memorandum by MR. ALEXANDER L. STOTT, page 73.

widen their job opportunities.[2] *We believe, however, that future efforts to improve the functioning of labor markets should not be limited to direct assistance to the disadvantaged but extend to all types of personnel.* In particular, much more emphasis should be placed on overcoming or preventing labor bottlenecks caused by critical skill shortages. In part, this should be achieved by gearing training and education more closely to developing job openings. We also believe there is need for heightened concern by business and government with the potentials for redesigning jobs to adapt them more effectively to the emerging changes in the country's labor supply. In addition, we urge greatly intensified efforts to eliminate existing discriminatory barriers to entry into particular types of jobs and professions.

There is an essential counterpart to sharply stepped-up efforts to enhance productivity and increase the flexibility and competitiveness of labor and product markets. If these efforts are to be successful, a much more active program must be developed to facilitate orderly adjustment to dynamic changes and prevent unnecessary hardships in the process of transition. Much of the existing resistance to change, including numerous restrictive labor and business practices, stems from fears of job and income losses. Such fears also give rise to wasteful government expenditures for the creation of unnecessary jobs. Many of these concerns are no longer justified in an economy basically committed to high employment and to providing specific protection against most of the major social and economic hazards. However, greater attention than heretofore must be given to the remaining risks that constitute legitimate sources of concern for many groups and individuals in our society.

In devising new efforts to foster productivity improvements and to cope constructively with the problems of adjusting to change, special attention should be given to the following approaches.

Productivity Bargaining. A mutual focus on productivity improvements and their implications needs to become a much more central feature of labor management relations. In this connection, use of "productivity bargaining" appears to be particularly promising. Such bargaining involves continuing cooperative efforts by management and labor to increase the efficiency of a firm's operations through changes in existing practices, coupled with agreements to assure an equitable shar-

---

[2] See *Training and Jobs for the Urban Poor* (July 1970), and *Education for the Urban Disadvantaged* (March 1971).

ing of the benefits as well as burdens of such changes. A condition in most productivity bargains has been that the desired changes would be put into effect only if actual displacement of workers could be kept to a minimum. Although these bargains have concentrated most frequently on the elimination of restrictive work rules, they can extend to a wide range of related matters as well—including job redesign, introduction of major technological changes, and use of profit sharing and other special incentive systems.

Experience in the United States and abroad suggests that the productivity bargaining approach has significant potential. Admittedly, use of this approach can also involve problems. Care has to be taken that the process does not lead to undue encroachments on management prerogatives. When productivity bargaining is used in conjunction with wage-price control programs, there is a risk that phony bargains will be developed to justify excessive wage increases.[3] Problems can also arise when genuine productivity bargains which lead to relatively large wage gains in one firm generate demands for comparable wage increases in other firms where an absence of restrictive practices has left no scope for such bargains.

On balance, however, it seems likely that the benefits from more extensive use of productivity bargaining will outweigh the potential drawbacks. The most important benefit is that this technique tends to place the main focus of labor-management relations on constructive joint approaches to the solution of mutual problems rather than solely on wages. **We therefore believe that strong efforts should be made to encourage increased reliance on the productivity bargaining technique in labor-management relations.** While such efforts must be carried out mainly by management and labor themselves, government can play a helpful role by identifying opportunities for such bargaining, by providing relevant information, and by other means.*

Innovative Techniques for Labor Market Improvements. Specific techniques for changing the general direction of labor market policies along the lines indicated above should include:

- Experimentation with a new type of public or nonprofit "Jobs Corporation" that would provide both training and jobs for mar-

---

[3]/On the other hand, control programs can also provide an opportunity to encourage genuine productivity bargaining to the extent that the control authorities put pressure on the parties involved to make joint efforts to hold down costs.

*See Memorandum by MR. HERMAN L. WEISS, page 73.

ginal and hard-core workers, as proposed in our 1970 policy statement, *Training and Jobs for the Urban Poor.* The principal purpose would be to link training more closely to the provision of job opportunities in both the private and public sectors.

• The development of more systematic programs concerned with fostering a more effective transition from school to work.

• The application of lower minimum wages than for other members of the labor force to the below-20 age group, the aged, and the partially disabled.

• The development of more effective programs to anticipate and cope with important skill shortages.

We also recommend federalization of the United States Employment Service and a major strengthening of its activities, including a significant further expansion and improvement in the use of computerized systems for matching job seekers and job vacancies. In our view, such a basic reform in the operation of this Service has attained growing urgency as labor markets have become increasingly interregional and even national in scope.*

A Broad Program to Aid Adjustments to Change. Productivity bargaining and general improvements in manpower planning and services can help significantly to reduce the adjustment problems posed for individuals and communities by advances in productivity and other dynamic changes in the economy. But in many cases some federal assistance may be required to cope with such problems, particularly where major and sudden dislocations are the result of the government's own actions and where workers have long past attachments to the labor force but not to specific firms. Scattered federal programs of adjustment assistance already exist. Some, for example, have been developed to ease the impact of reductions in trade barriers and of sudden cutbacks in military spending; recently, special programs were developed to aid unemployed engineers and scientists affected by such cutbacks. Many of these measures, however, have been carried out on an *ad hoc* basis only, after crises had already emerged.

We recommend that existing adjustment assistance programs be consolidated and made part of a much more comprehensive and integrated national program to facilitate adjustment to rapid economic

---

*See Memorandum by MR. HERMAN L. WEISS, page 74.

changes and to provide reasonable assistance to those threatened with major hardships as a result of such changes. The scope of any new national program of this type should be carefully delineated to avoid unjustified subsidies. On the other hand, estimates of its cost will need to take account of the potential savings from steps that serve to overcome resistance to changes which are needed to render our economy more competitive and productive. Among the measures that should be considered is the creation of a federally-administered national manpower readjustment fund. The primary purpose of this fund would be to provide special income assistance as well as added training, job search, and relocation financing for displaced workers who meet the requirements of the program but are ineligible for adequate assistance under present programs. Much fuller consideration also needs to be given to possible means of increasing the transferability of pension rights and other fringe benefits.* In addition, other steps in the area of pension reform may well be desirable, including measures to require appropriate vesting provisions in private pension plans.

Strengthening Competition in Product and Labor Markets

Another broad task for structural reforms must be to reduce the many rigidities and imperfections in our product and labor markets that interfere with the proper working of competitive forces and cause prices and costs to be less responsive to downward than to upward pressures.

A great many of these rigidities are based on outmoded laws and regulatory practices. *We reiterate our earlier recommendation that a major and comprehensive review of existing statutes, regulations and practices be undertaken to "eliminate depression-born features that have an inherent inflationary bias, work counter to efficiency and resource mobility, and are inappropriate for a high employment economy."* A central organizational mechanism is needed to translate the results of such a review into specific programs for reform. Adoption of this procedure should not mean years of delay before anything is done. In many areas, much of the required information is already available, and the need is to bring proposals for action to the forefront of governmental and public attention.

---

*See Memorandum by MR. ALEXANDER L. STOTT, page 74.

Steps required to overcome legal and other structural impediments to price flexibility in *product markets* include especially:

- Enforcement of the antitrust laws in ways which give particular emphasis to assuring the responsiveness of the price system to competitive forces, but with due allowance for mergers which in fact increase productivity and competition.*

- Elimination or modification of various legal provisions that place undesirable floors under prices, including a gradual shift from relatively high farm price supports to more direct forms of assistance, as well as removal of various requirements for price maintenance at retail that add appreciably to consumer living costs.**

- A vigorous and comprehensive effort to curtail other direct and indirect subsidies and output restrictions that raise prices unduly and interfere with efficient resource allocation. In many instances, of course, the use of subsidies can serve desirable social objectives. But far more needs to be done to identify clearly the full range of subsidies and to assure that decisions on their continuance are based on an accurate assessment of their impact on prices as well as on budgetary costs.

- Modification or elimination of overly detailed and inflexible rate regulations in industries such as surface transportation, and more active exploration of the scope for increased reliance on market-type incentives in other regulated industries.

- Further reductions in existing barriers to the unimpeded movement of international trade and investment. In some instances, of course, valid reasons exist for retaining restrictions, particularly where these are needed on national security grounds. It is especially vital, however, that recent intensified pressures for the widespread use of mandatory import quotas and other protectionist measures be firmly resisted. Adoption of such measures would run wholly counter to the pressing current need for overcoming inflationary forces and increasing the economy's productivity.

Efforts to overcome competitive imbalances and restrictive practices in *labor markets* must, in our view, constitute a key feature in any program for structural reform. *We again urge that a basic restructuring*

---

*See Memorandum by MR. HERMAN L. WEISS, page 74.
**See Memorandum by MR. HERMAN L. WEISS, page 74.

50.

of labor laws and regulations be undertaken to bring about a better balance in the relative powers of unions and management. The existence of strong and active unions is vitally important for the proper functioning of our economy, and the basic right of labor to organize and bargain collectively must be fully protected. Corrective action is needed, however, in the many instances where the application of labor laws—originally developed when unions were weak—now results in clearly excessive union powers.*

Among the types of reform that we have advocated in the past and on which early action continues to be highly desirable are the following:[4]

- A strengthening of existing legal and administrative provisions to assure the elimination of racial, sex, and other discriminatory barriers to union membership, apprenticeship, or employment.

- Prohibition of political contributions by unions as well as by corporations in those states which do not now have such restraints.

- Tightening existing legal rules against secondary boycotts and coercive picketing.

- Clarification by law rather than by *ad hoc* rulings of what constitutes a statutory duty to bargain.

- Protection of employers' right to communicate freely with employees as long as such "free speech" is not coercive.

- Assurance that disputes over unfair labor practices are handled in a more judicial fashion than at present.

- Prohibition of the payment of unemployment insurance benefits to strikers in those states where such a practice is now permitted.**

In addition, the emergency procedures of the Taft-Hartley Act should provide for more options than are now available.[5]

---

[4]/For earlier recommendations in this area, see particularly *Union Powers and Union Functions* (March 1964), and *Further Weapons Against Inflation* (November 1970).

[5]/A variety of special approaches also needs to be developed to cope with the structural problems of particular industries or sectors where inflationary pressures have been especially severe, notably construction and medical care. For discussion and recommendations concerning the special problems of the construction sector, see *Further Weapons Against Inflation* (November 1970), pp. 48-51. Our Subcommittee on the Organization and Financing of a National Health Care System is currently examining the scope for basic reforms in the health services field.

*See Memorandum by MR. PHILIP SPORN, page 74.

**See Memorandum by MR. HERMAN L. WEISS, page 75.

National Emergency Strike Procedures

A particularly serious impediment to the proper functioning of market processes and the prevention of inflation is posed by the threat or actual use of major strikes. Since these often have gravely disruptive effects on all or large segments of the nation's economy, there is urgent need for more effective procedures to deal with them.

The right to strike has long been regarded as an essential ingredient of the free collective bargaining process in the private sector. We do not believe this right should be restricted except in cases where the strike would have such crippling effects as to produce serious emergencies. In some instances major or prolonged strikes impose crippling effects on large sections of the economy and on wide segments of the public, thereby producing pressures for settlement that become so great as to remove any really effective resistance to unreasonable demands. In such cases, eagerness to end the strike leads all too often to a readiness to accept "peace at any price." And the price is usually a shift of the costs to the public. This problem has become more and more serious as the growing complexity and interrelatedness of our modern economy has rendered large-scale disruptions of economic activity increasingly intolerable to the public.

While existing labor laws provide limited remedies for the problems of national emergency labor disputes,[6] there is clear need for improving the existing machinery for coping with national emergency strikes. A more orderly procedure for resolving disputes after the expiration of initial "cooling-off" periods should replace the present tendency to leave such matters to *ad hoc* determination by the Congress. Efforts to cope with this problem involve a basic dilemma, however: the cure may be even worse than the disease. There is a major danger that an expectation of an eventual governmentally-imposed solution will merely cause the parties to refrain from genuine collective bargaining and leave determination of most final settlements entirely up to governmental arbitrators. It could mean too frequent governmental interference in labor-management disputes which could add to the fuels of inflation. When the disputes have been turned over to compulsory arbitration or Congressional determination, the eagerness to show results in ending the strike has very often led to especially inflationary settlements.

---

[6] Separate types of remedies are provided under the Taft-Hartley Act and the Railway Labor Act. For a brief description and assessment of these two statutes, see Appendix.

The Administration has recently made a series of proposals for improving present procedures for resolving national emergency labor disputes. These proposals would initially apply only in the transportation industries, where the problem of crippling strikes has been most serious, but might eventually be applicable on a wider basis. Essentially, they would supplement existing procedures provided by the Taft-Hartley Act and also make the new procedures applicable to situations now covered by the Railway Labor Act. The proposals are designed to maximize rather than reduce incentives for genuine collective bargaining at every stage. This is because the process would leave the parties relatively uncertain as to what the final method of resolving the impasse would prove to be.

Under these proposals, the President would be able to invoke *one* of three options for settling the dispute after the cooling-off period has expired: first, a thirty-day extension of the cooling-off period; second, a provision for partial operation of the industry for a maximum period of up to 180 days, following a finding by a special board that this would be consistent with national health and safety; and third, the use of a "final offer selection" procedure.

Under the latter procedure, each of the parties would have to submit a final offer to the Secretary of Labor. If the issue was not resolved after a further mandatory period of bargaining, a special Final Offer Selection Board would choose one of the offers, without alteration, as the one that would be binding on the two parties.

Since under these proposals neither party would know which option the President might choose among those available to him, mere delay in making a reasonable offer would not necessarily be to its advantage. The final offer selection procedure, moreover, is designed to provide further incentives for narrowing the differences between the offers. It would also minimize the scope for governmental intervention since the arbitrators cannot make any changes in the offers but are merely able to choose one of those submitted. These techniques, it is thought, would overcome the difficulties encountered under the usual types of compulsory arbitration which give wide leeway to arbitrators and encourage the two sides to adopt extreme positions—all too often leading the arbitrator to simply "split the difference."

We believe that a package-of-options approach would constitute a change in the right direction. We feel, however, that improved emergency strike procedures must go further than those now under consideration if they are to address themselves adequately to the inflationary threat rather than merely to the prevention of strikes. A major drawback under most existing proposals is the likelihood that the public interest in price stability will not be sufficiently considered when disputes are finally resolved. This can be a drawback under the final offer selection procedure, just as under other types of compulsory arbitration.

We therefore recommend that a "package-of-options" procedure be adopted as a supplement to the existing Taft-Hartley Act and Railway Labor Act provisions for handling national emergency strikes— a procedure along lines like those just outlined but with a major addition. In making their final offers, the two parties should be asked to take into account the likely effect on price stability, and the Final Offer Selection Board should be required to reject both offers if they appeared to be strongly inflationary in nature. In such cases, the two parties should be obligated to submit a new set of final offers. During periods when final offers were being developed, strikes would continue to be enjoined.

These procedures should not be used except in cases where major damage to national health or safety is involved. Although initially they might be limited to the transportation sector, consideration should be given to their use in other industries as well.

Resort to "impasse resolution" procedures that involve elements of government compulsion is, of course, far less desirable than the use of arbitration procedures to which the two parties agree on a voluntary basis. We, therefore, urge that when impasse situations arise, labor and management make every effort to rely on voluntary arbitration to the fullest extent possible.

6.

Containing Inflationary Forces and Raising Productivity in the Public Sector

Aₙ IMPORTANT SOURCE of inflationary pressures in the economy is the way in which governments at all levels conduct many of their own operations. Federal, state and local governments in the aggregate account for approximately 22 per cent of the gross national product and in combination they are the largest employer. In some areas of activity, moreover, the direct governmental role is particularly large. For example, public construction has accounted for nearly one-half of all nonresidential construction in recent years.

The Need for an Integrated Approach. The range of governmental activities that can affect the price structure is extraordinarily wide. It includes government purchasing and procurement policies; construction operations; the administration of stockpile reserves and of numerous subsidy programs; the use of regulations that require agencies to give preference to domestic rather than foreign suppliers; the management of programs of grants-in-aid to other levels of government; the administration of various regulatory activities; and the setting of wages for almost 13 million civilian government employees.

The great bulk of such activities was carried out until recently without an integrated and conscious concern about their effect on over-all price stability. In our 1970 policy statement, *Further Weapons Against Inflation,* we recommended that at the national level, a central governmental unit be given strong powers to act as a "public defender" of the price stability objective within the federal government. Such a unit should concentrate continuously and exclusively on reducing or averting inflationary pressures associated with government operations. Since this recommendation was made, the interagency Regulations and Purchasing Review Board has enlarged the scope of its functions so that it could carry out the type of integrating role that we proposed. The price effects of governmental operations, of course, have also received significant attention from the Price Commission and the Cost of Living Council. But these efforts fall far short of what is required.

We recommend that existing efforts to develop an integrated approach toward minimizing the inflationary potentials of the federal government's operations be substantially strengthened and be followed up by more vigorous action. The powers and activities of the Regulations and Purchasing Review Board should be significantly expanded. In this connection, we reiterate our earlier recommendation that the Board be required to estimate and make public the likely impact on the general price level of significant new legislative and other proposals for governmental action—including, among others, proposals for new spending programs, subsidies, and trade restrictions.

Although the procedures outlined here would mainly be directed at federal government activities, they should also have considerable influence on state and local government practices because of the widespread use of federal grants-in-aid, loans, guarantees, etc. Similar procedures might well be adopted by state governments as a means of holding down their costs as well as those of local governments.

But the task of minimizing inflationary potentials of government operations involves far more problems than can be assigned to any one board or commission. In particular, greatly intensified efforts are required to increase productivity at all levels of government. There is also a pressing need for basic improvements in government labor-management relations and wage-determination processes.

Our Committee has dealt with many aspects of these and related issues in prior policy statements, particularly those concerned with improving management in the government sector. As we have already indicated, however, extraordinarily serious fiscal problems currently face the federal government as well as state and local governments. There is also the danger that rising costs may increasingly weaken the quality and adequacy of needed public services. In light of this situation, we believe it is essential that extensive additional attention be devoted to ways of containing inflationary pressures in the public sector. For this reason, we are now embarking on a new study that will focus specifically on governmental productivity and employee compensation. Consequently, no attempt will be made here to spell out the full range of reforms that are called for. Instead, the remainder of this chapter highlights the nature of some of the key problems that need to be faced.

Raising Government Productivity. The task of raising productivity in the public sector has many dimensions. It should involve far-reaching reforms in the structure and processes of governments at all levels, in particular the reduction of the fragmentation and overlapping that now exists.[1] It calls for greater reliance on better management techniques, including especially program budgeting, long-range comprehensive planning, and cost-effectiveness evaluation.[2] It requires substantial improvements in professional education for public service and greater willingness to make use of professionally trained managers.

There is also a need to develop productivity measures applicable to the public sector. The recent development of a productivity index covering over half of federal government activities represents a major step in this direction. Similar measures are needed for state and local government services, including education. Throughout the public sector, there is need to identify especially promising possibilities for productivity improvement and to pursue vigorously the changes required to realize them. Much greater emphasis also needs to be placed on the introduction of market-type incentives wherever feasible, as well as on fuller use of private sector capabilities through contracting and other means.

---

[1]/For specific recommendations, see *Making Congress More Effective* (September 1970), *A Fiscal Program for a Balanced Federalism* (June 1967), *Modernizing State Government* (July 1967), *Reshaping Government in Metropolitan Areas* (February 1970), *Modernizing Local Government* (July 1966).

[2]/See *Improving Federal Program Performance* (September 1971).

Wage Determination in the Public Sector. Over the last decade, average earnings in the public sector have risen significantly faster than those in the private sector. In part, this has reflected the fact that as demands for public sector services grew, the granting of above-average wage increases served as one means of attracting additional labor resources to that sector.[3] But numerous other influences have also been at work. Thus, from 1956 to 1970 union membership in the public sector more than doubled in absolute numbers while there was virtually no growth in private sector union membership. At the same time, public sector unions have become substantially more militant, as evidenced by the surge in public sector strikes.

The unusually rapid increase in public sector earnings during recent years also has stemmed from the influence of a wide range of legally-mandated procedures to assure comparability of public and private compensation. In considerable measure, lagging public sector wage and fringe benefit rates have now caught up with private sector compensation levels. Indeed, for some categories of government workers, public compensation recently has moved well ahead of private compensation. This is particularly true when account is taken of the fact that a number of cities now provide extremely liberal pension arrangements for an increasing number of employees that permit retirement on full pension, regardless of age, after twenty years' service.

Some of the pressures which recently have produced the rapid wage increases in the public sector should abate in the near future. Partly as a result of population trends, for example, there has been a slowdown of the growth in the demand for teachers, which accounted for the largest share of the postwar rise in governmental employment. Moreover, as we have indicated, the process of achieving pay comparability appears to have been completed for many public employees.

Nevertheless, there are strong reasons for continuing concern with the potential inflationary pressures associated with wage determination in the public sector. A primary reason is that governmental wage setting is not subject to the same type and degree of restraining influences that are associated with private bargaining. Thus, collective bargaining is very often conducted by elected officials whose political future is influenced by the compensation decisions involved. Moreover,

---

[3] Although federal employment has declined as a share of total employment in recent decades, state and local government employment has almost doubled its share in the postwar period.

wage and benefit determination may be based on various legally-mandated procedures that can serve as independent sources of inflationary pressures.

It is also important to realize that the outcome of public sector wage settlements has a key bearing on the fiscal situation of governments at all levels and can exert important bellwether effects on private sector bargaining. Furthermore, to the extent that public sector wage increases are reflected in higher taxes and rising charges for public services, living costs for all workers are increased. This, in turn, can add to wage demands in the private sector.

Efforts to minimize possible inflationary consequences of the wage-setting process in the public sector require action particularly in the following areas:

1. *Developing Better Techniques to Determine Pay Comparability.* As already noted, the compensation of many public employees is based either by statute or regulation on surveys of "comparability" with the private sector. This is especially true for federal government workers but also applies to many state and local employees covered by legally-mandated prevailing wage procedures. While we continue to favor the principle of comparability of governmental and private pay, we believe that the methods for determining comparability may now be resulting in excessive compensation for some groups of public employees. At the federal level, for example, there is a possibility that the exclusion of certain types of companies from the comparability surveys is a factor giving an upward bias to the survey results. In comparability determinations, considerably more also needs to be known about the proper role of fringe benefits and regularity of employment. Several investigations of such problems are now under way, mostly within the federal government. However, further appraisals are needed to assess the merits of the techniques currently being used to determine pay comparability as well as to develop improved procedures for assuring that comparability systems do not operate as engines of inflation.

2. *Improving Collective Bargaining Processes.* In states and localities where collective bargaining is used to determine public employee compensation, wide scope exists for improvements in the nature of this process. The legal rights and obligations of the parties concerned often should be more clearly delineated. Many local govern-

ments, moreover, are inexperienced in collective bargaining techniques and should devote substantial additional resources to develop adequate professional expertise in personnel management and labor relations. It is particularly important for such local governments to explore more fully the possibilities for bringing productivity and efficiency more explicitly into the collective bargaining process.

3. *Reducing Wage-Spiral Effects of Public Sector Bargaining.* An upward spiral in labor costs can develop at the municipal and state levels when an excessive wage settlement in one locality sets the pattern for demands in other localities. Frequently, the fact that public officials sit at one side of the bargaining table is not a sufficient guarantee that there will be proper representation of the broader public interest in avoiding clearly inflationary agreements. Nor does this fact guarantee that proper account will be taken of the more direct interests of the federal and state governments which frequently end up paying the bill. It is clearly desirable to develop more effective means of dealing with such deficiencies. One possible approach would be to broaden the size of bargaining units to avoid "whipsawing" of smaller jurisdictions. In at least one state, consideration is already being given to a system of statewide bargaining. An additional moderating influence might be a more systematic effort by the federal government and by state governments to take some account of the degree of local government compliance with the national wage-price guidelines when they are considering new grants, loans, and other forms of assistance.

4. *Developing Alternatives to Strikes of Government Employees.* Pressures for excessive wage increases in the public sector can become particularly intense when they are accompanied by strikes that represent a serious threat to public health or safety. For the most part, strikes are legally prohibited in the public sector. For this reason, however, development of improved procedures is particularly necessary to resolve impasses in public sector collective bargaining, especially at the state and local levels. The procedures under the Taft-Hartley Act, as well as the additional techniques recommended in Chapter 5, generally apply only to actual or potential strikes that create nationwide emergencies. Thus, in many states and localities there is need to evolve measures to cope with strikes of public employees which could create local emergencies.

Reconciling Economic Measures
and Political Realities

As we indicated in the introduction to this statement, political difficulties stand in the way of most of the steps we are recommending. But to rule out any one category of measures on the ground that it is "politically impossible" of achievement is likely to put most of the remaining burden on other sets of measures that may in practice be equally difficult to implement. Moreover, each failure to seek needed but unpopular structural reforms—such as elimination of restrictive labor or management practices that impede productivity, reduction of trade restrictions, or removal of unnecessary government subsidies—tends to place increased stress on the use of direct controls over prices and wages. This can be expected to occur even though in the long run such controls may be even less palatable to the public at large.

In a very real sense, therefore, those who claim that needed innovations in fiscal and monetary management or in the structural area are politically unfeasible may be presenting the American public with an unacceptable proposition. In effect, they may be asking American workers and businessmen to submit to far greater restraints on their freedom of action than are desirable (or can be sustained) over the longer run.

None of the choices is easy; almost all involve some serious drawbacks and inequities. We are hopeful, however, that if the American public obtains a clear picture of the full range of choices facing the nation, it will choose those measures that will be most in the public interest.

Memoranda of Comment, Reservation, or Dissent

Page 10—By ROBERT B. SEMPLE:

In this paper there are so many proposals and "rules," and so many schemes and modifications thereof for administering and "fine tuning" the economy in an effort to counter departures from basic economic theory that I wonder if we have not lost the keys to attaining the rather ill defined goals we seek—much less the interim target of 4% unemployment with 2% inflation.

Merely exhorting our various sectors to strive for more productivity will not solve the problem of inflation. Nor will improved education, a National Commission on Productivity, or a "Jobs Corporation." It will undoubtedly always be true that productivity will grow at varying rates in different industries and between groups, especially the service sectors vs. manufacturing. In some, it will not grow at all—it still takes 100 musicians to perform a symphonic composition written in the nineteenth century just as it did then. A key economic principle is that the benefits of enhanced productivity that are not attributable to a person's own physical or mental effort should be passed on as a fair return on the capital used to gain the increase, and in the form of lower prices. When monopoly powers of groups prevent this lowering of prices, but take all the productivity gain, and more, for themselves, we have an inflationary tendency.

This is so because there must be some relevance between the earning power of our various groups; otherwise our social schemes and remedies come into play with legislated minimum wages, price supports, payments to the unemployed, etc. The unemployed would be employable at a living wage if those with monopoly powers had not priced them out of the market for both jobs and the purchase of goods and services. I find our prescriptions for dealing with these problems inadequate and lacking in detail.

Page 10—By ALLAN SPROUL, with which C. WREDE PETERSMEYER has asked to be associated. FRAZAR B. WILDE has also asked to be associated, especially with the last paragraph:

This is a fine Statement of its kind, but it is not the kind of Statement which responds to the urgency of the problem of getting rid of Phase II of the New Economic Program as quickly as possible, without reverting to the kind of situation which made Phase II necessary.

It contains an overload of recommendations and suggestions, in which individual proposals get lost despite their possible merits, complex subjects are given cursory treatment, hard choices are passed on for further study, dubious new government entities are tentatively proposed, and the impact of the document as an answer to an urgent present need is seriously diluted.

The urgent present need is to create a situation in which existing wage, price, dividend and profit margin controls can be dismantled as soon as they have served their temporary purpose, so that we may return with some assurance to a primarily market process of achieving high employment without inflation.

Given the political dynamite contained in the present and prospective constellation of prices and employment, there is a danger that political pressures will inhibit the adoption of appropriate fiscal policies and the administration of appropriate monetary policies, both of which will be needed if there is not to be a revival of inflationary pressures from the demand side as the upsurge in the economy moves ahead. In such a climate the expectation of continuing inflation, which has bedevilled wage and price behavior in recent years, and which has been muted but not banished by the New Economic Policy, will gain a new lease on life.

This danger must be opposed by the monetary authorities, who will have to tread a narrow path between supplying the reserve funds needed for vigorous economic growth and avoiding the oversupply which would fuel excess demand, and it must be opposed by the executive and legislative branches of the federal government in terms of restraint on government spending and in terms of providing increased revenues through increased taxes when that becomes necessary. In addition to appropriate fiscal and monetary policies, however, we also shall have need of a direct and effective government influence on the cost-push inflationary pressures in the economy.

The direct and vital way to gain such an influence, without a panoply of government controls, is by a positive assertion of government authority in our collective bargaining arrangements, which have too often been the handmaiden of excessive wage demands and price increases.

The most promising suggestion for meeting this need is a proposal already put forward by the government (in a special case) for the imposition of a "final offer selection" procedure in collective bargaining, a proposal which is given favorable notice in Chapter 5 of this Statement, but in a partial and apologetic way.

In my opinion the Statement should endorse this mandatory form of government compulsion, to be applied permanently over a wide spectrum of the economy and without genuflections toward voluntary controls. This would be a significant change in our institutional arrangements, but it would be a change less foreign to our general style of economic life than long continued wage, price, dividend and profit margin controls. If there is to be a prompt dismantling of Phase II of the New Economic Policy, some such institutional change is necessary. Failure directly to tackle the cost-push aspect of inflation in our economy can make the expectation of inflation and inflation itself inevitable.

Page 14—By JOHN D. HARPER:

It is a gross understatement to say that traditional policy prescriptions have not been followed during some crucial periods; in the years 1965-68 they were seldom, if ever, followed. The result was the fueling of a substantial inflation, and inflationary psychology, which fully erupted in subsequent years. If we have learned anything at all about our economy in recent years, we should now recognize that it is extremely difficult to curb rising prices in a large complex, industrialized economy once woefully inadequate aggregate demand policies have permitted inflation to get under way and accelerate. It seems to me that this entire statement is built on the premise that since aggregate demand policies have not brought satisfactory results, we ought to supplement them with some form of wage-price policies that will somehow compensate for massive prior mistakes in fiscal and monetary policies. I am still strongly opposed to any form of incomes policy or controls program, as stated in my comments on pages 78-79 in the November 1970 Policy Statement *Further Weapons Against Inflation*. Nevertheless, even though I disagree with the basic premise on which this current statement is based, I am forced to go along with it because a number of very excellent proposals are included, particularly the comments regarding the importance of profits in Chapter 4, as well as the structural reforms for the private sector cited in Chapter 5 and for the public sector in Chapter 6.

Page 14—By JOHN D. HARPER:

The statement that "the desired dampening of aggregate demand was for a time substantially less pronounced than had been anticipated" appears to represent the viewpoint of the so-called fiscalists. The result was precisely what the monetarists believed would occur, particularly since the money supply was expanded rapidly in the latter half of 1968. It may well be that the rise in unemployment during 1970-71 was larger than expected, but certainly nowhere near all of it resulted from the demand contraction. A substantial portion was due to winding down the Vietnam War with the resulting layoffs in defense-oriented industries and returning veterans.

Page 15—By JOHN D. HARPER, with which C. WREDE PETERSMEYER has asked to be associated:

No one can deny that by mid-1971 some people felt that stronger medicine was required to curb inflationary forces. However, the facts simply do not support the statement that these forces were gathering momentum. By mid-1971 the annual rate of inflation in consumer prices (comparing the percentage change in the Consumer Price Index from the same month a year earlier) had been declining systematically and substantially since early 1970. This point is forcefully demonstrated by Milton Friedman in his *Newsweek* article of May 22, 1972, page 86.

Page 16—By MARVIN BOWER, with which STEWART S. CORT, JOHN J. HARPER, JOHN A. PERKINS, C. WREDE PETERSMEYER, and SIDNEY J. WEINBERG, JR. have asked to be associated:

The degree of the nation's "will" (or resolve) is the determining factor. Unless the electorate and its leaders and legislators show a greater willingness than they are showing currently to pay for public services and benefits on a more current basis, and so avoid large and continuous budget deficits, then neither fiscal nor monetary policy nor any number of control phases will be successful in avoiding a high rate of (or even runaway) inflation. History shows that control of inflation depends ultimately on the character of the people and their capacity for self-denial.

Even the will of Congress is impeded by present congressional procedures which do not provide for totalling the expenditures approved during a session. This deficiency was discussed in earlier CED policy statements, *Budgeting for National Objectives* (1966) and *Making Congress More Effective* (1970).

Page 16—By JOHN D. HARPER:

Rather than call appropriate fiscal and monetary policies a central ingredient, I would call them *the* central ingredient for achieving high level prosperity without inflation.

Page 16—By FRANKLIN A. LINDSAY:

In addition to the sound management of total demand through general fiscal and monetary policies, consideration should be given to more specific influences on demand in key sectors of the economy. When, as a by-product of efforts to control inflation, general monetary and fiscal policies cause serious underutilization of existing productive capacity in any key sector, the results can be to slow or stop economic growth and to increase unemployment in that sector, thereby generating added inflationary forces as well as deflationary pressures.

In order to escape the dilemma of either *price stability, under-employment, and low growth* or *high employment, high growth and inflation,* we should now move toward a policy of treating separately certain broad areas of the economy by use of specialized economic controls and incentives which can be applied selectively to each of these sectors. Through such a sectoral approach it should be possible to bring about, in a few key sectors, levels of employment and plant utilization which are closer to capacity and to introduce some greater stability in growth so that new capacity will be added without encouraging the feast-or-famine cycle in investment resulting first from inflationary expectations followed by stringent capital controls.

The government has begun to back into such a sectoral approach with a broad variety of specialized credit devices specifically for the housing industry. In addition to housing, other broad areas of capital investment such as highways and mass transportation, electric power, communications, water supply and pollution control may be amenable to sectoral management through specialized fiscal and monetary devices.

It should be possible to apply a few carefully designed incentives and controls effectively to a few broad areas of the economy where overall long-term needs can be forecast with reasonable accuracy, while at the same time leaving specific price and investment decisions within these sectors to the free and competitive action of the market. Further, if high and stable growth and full use of productive capacity are achieved in those sectors, high growth, full employment, and price stability are more likely to result in the rest of the economy.

Page 17—By JOHN D. HARPER:

We don't really know whether or not this statement is true, inasmuch as inadequate monetary-fiscal policies during 1965-68 caused rapidly rising prices, cost-push pressures, and a build-up in inflationary psychology. It may well be that with improved management of total demand there would have been no cost-push inflationary influence to contain.

Page 17—By JOHN D. HARPER:

In addition to labor and product markets, the services sector should also be mentioned as being subject to essential reform.

Page 17—By JOHN D. HARPER, with which C. WREDE PETERSMEYER has asked to be associated:

As indicated earlier, I continue to reject any form of incomes policy as being the answer, or even a partial answer, to curbing inflation in this country. Even if a convincing case could be made on economic grounds (which it cannot) that an incomes policy might help to restrain inflation, the danger of paving the way for more government intervention in our economic system does not warrant taking the risk in the first place. It seems to me that all such wage-price policy proposals are essentially anti-market oriented no matter how innocent they appear to be on the surface. In my view the impersonal market mechanism will always perform better and more efficiently than a command system operated by government officials.

Page 17—By HERMAN L. WEISS, with which JOHN D. HARPER has asked to be associated:

I do not believe the paper develops a case sufficiently persuasive to support the assertion that demand and structural measures will have to be supplemented for the foreseeable future with wage-price (or incomes) policies. This statement seems to make an assumption that the nation will fail to invoke effective demand and structural measures to control inflation.

Page 18—By MARVIN BOWER, with which JOHN J. HARPER and C. WREDE PETERSMEYER have asked to be associated:

I am not convinced that "over the longer run" wage and price controls can be effective in an economy as large and complex as ours, except during a time of all-out war. At least it would require the will or resolve to which I referred in my earlier footnote in Chapter 1; and if that is present in an adequate degree, wage and price controls would not be needed.

Page 18—By JOHN D. HARPER, with which C. WREDE PETERSMEYER has asked to be associated:

As indicated earlier, I cannot agree that direct governmental concern with wage and price decisions is desirable over the longer run since I also reject governmental intervention with the market mechanism in the short run.

Nor do I believe that statutory authority for compulsory controls should be continued on a standby basis. Through proper use of its broad indirect measures, namely fiscal and monetary policies, the government has ample power to maintain high employment without inflation. Obviously, this will involve difficult choices for policy makers in the Administration and for members of the Congress. The responsibility for inflation is theirs; it does not lie with the actions of either labor or business.

Page 18—By HERMAN L. WEISS, with which JOHN D. HARPER has asked to be associated:

I do not think a sound case has been made for the need for compulsory controls on a standby basis. On the contrary, I think such standby measures would make it too easy for the politicians to avoid and delay the tough decisions that are required to deal effectively with both structural and demand-pull problems.

Page 21—By HERMAN L. WEISS:

While there may be a few instances of "spillover" effects from wage increases in manufacturing industries, the evidence suggests that the *reverse* has been the more general case in recent years.

Page 22—By JOHN D. HARPER, with which C. WREDE PETERSMEYER and HERMAN L. WEISS have asked to be associated:

The implications in this sentence appear to me to be wrong in two ways. First, if one believes in the market system, why should any firm forego price increases if supply-demand conditions and competitive factors permit them? Second, I submit that firms do institute price cuts when markets weaken. Actual prices are much more flexible in the marketplace than most government officials and academic economists realize. While it is true that book or list prices for products in manufacturing change infrequently, the reverse is true for actual transaction prices. About one-third of the Bureau of Labor Statistics' Wholesale Price Index is made up of list prices provided by sellers, not actual prices paid by buyers. We need, but do not have, a good price index that would show the extent to which actual transaction prices do fluctuate in the marketplace. Contrary to a good deal of mistaken belief, prices fluctuate widely in the marketplace throughout manufacturing and are not rigid or inflexible downward when demand weakens. The ability of firms, large or small, to administer their prices against the forces of the market is highly exaggerated. If this were not so, why have profit margins on sales by American manufacturers been so low in recent years.

68.

Page 22—By HERMAN L. WEISS, with which JOHN D. HARPER has asked to be associated:

This paragraph completely ignores the fact that companies in the electrical, copper and can industries took long strikes in order to resist excessive wage demands. And some companies in other industries which were too weak or without capital capabilities to take strikes found they were not able to maintain the higher prices they tried to get in the wake of excessive wage settlements (e. g. steel).

Page 23—By JOHN D. HARPER:

Once again I must object to direct governmental intervention in the process of wage and price determination. Also, as pointed out earlier, the inflation rate, using the Consumer Price Index as a measure, had been trending downward for a year and a half prior to the imposition of the control program in August 1971.

Page 31—By MARVIN BOWER, with which JOHN A. PERKINS and C. WREDE PETERSMEYER have asked to be associated:

The record is still pretty sketchy that any administration will show the political courage to balance the budget or develop a surplus at a time when the "rules" call for this action. In other words, there is a risk that the "rules" will be used as a rationalization for a continuously unbalanced budget.

Page 33—By ALEXANDER L. STOTT:

When this recommendation was made in an earlier Policy Statement in 1969, I objected to it on the grounds that frequent tax changes have a disruptive effect on business planning and performance. It may be difficult or expensive to change business expansion plans, and changes in earnings of regulated businesses may require rate action by regulatory authorities. I believe that these objections are still valid today, and suggest that, wherever possible, the objectives of greater fiscal flexibility be sought through more careful budgetary reviews, including the anticipated future effects of existing and proposed federal programs, and through changes in proposed federal spending.

Page 35—By ALLAN SPROUL:

Trying to extend the range and impact of government influence on the allocation of economic resources by selective credit controls, or by credit rationing, would be a plunge into a thicket of social and political pressures which could debauch overall monetary policy.

*Page 36—*By ALEXANDER L. STOTT:

CED's earlier statement on selective controls largely involved measures to strengthen sectors which were adversely affected by monetary restraint, but did not seem to go as far as this statement does in suggesting "selective measures . . . that impinge directly on other sectors." Because these new measures are not spelled out, and because such measures may produce side effects that are more undesirable than the problems which they are intended to correct, I cannot agree that such measures ". . . may prove useful."

*Page 36—*By ALEXANDER L. STOTT:

The undesirable effects on business plans and growth of a stop-and-go policy on major tax incentives greatly reduce the value of these measures as long-range stimuli to economic growth, and involve serious difficulty for business where expansion plans frequently involve long lead times and cannot be readily changed. While this suggestion is not technically a recommendation, it is nevertheless made as a leading suggestion for consideration, and I feel it is a poor example to cite for further study. The concession, later in the paragraph, that there are drawbacks to frequent changes in the investment credit, adds to the impression that the Policy Statement could have included some more reasonable suggestions than only the one given here.

*Page 36—*By HERMAN L. WEISS:

I have reservations about the variable investment tax credit. What this provision would do, in effect, would be to give the government even more power to allocate capital resources. It would be unfortunate to have a situation where government agencies would have the right to decide when and where it would be desirable to have capital assets replaced.

*Page 37—*By JOHN D. HARPER:

As pointed out earlier, I cannot agree with the premise that improved management of overall demand will not be sufficient to reconcile high employment and price stability. Admittedly, we have not been able to manage overall demand with sufficient skill to really test the premise. Nevertheless, it seems to me that both the Administration's policy makers and the Congress should begin to accept their responsibility for causing inflation and make the hard choices necessary to stabilize the economy.

Page 38—By JOHN D. HARPER:

As mentioned previously, I do not believe that voluntary wage-price restraints are either appropriate or effective since they deal only with symptoms and not the causes of inflation. While policy makers in Washington felt that a strong case for compulsory controls existed in 1971, it is difficult to find any evidence to support their case. Furthermore, rather than contain the process of distortion brought on by the earlier excessive demand inflation, I believe that the controls will lead to much worse distortions in our economy the longer they are continued.

Page 39—By JOHN D. HARPER, with which C. WREDE PETERSMEYER has asked to be associated:

I must repeatedly reject the idea that wage and price decisions are a cause of inflation. Improper use of demand management tools is the culprit and the responsibility should be placed correctly on those who have mismanaged monetary and fiscal policies. Relying on voluntary cooperation by labor and business will have little or no effect on the inflation rate and compulsory controls are completely objectionable.

Page 39—By HERMAN L. WEISS, with which STEWART S. CORT and JOHN D. HARPER have asked to be associated:

The primary need over the long run is to maintain some orderly mechanism for systematic correction of structural problems and for the prompt application of fiscal-monetary measures. This mechanism would get to the *causes* of inflation in contrast to the *symptoms* which are the primary targets of either voluntary or compulsory controls.

Page 39—By HERMAN L. WEISS:

This exemption is highly controversial and there is nothing in the report to support an endorsement of it.

Page 39—By HERMAN L. WEISS:

This sentence, in effect, suggests that an industry may be de-controlled provided it exhibits the right behavior on profitability. The implication is that stable or declining profits provide the kind of evidence that would permit the government to de-control prices. This plus the reference to a "legally required norm" are the types of statements which strongly imply profit control.

Page 40—By JOHN D. HARPER:

In this entire paragraph I gain the impression that rising prices are somehow bad and where this occurs controls should not be lifted. It should be remembered that price changes perform a valuable function in signaling changes in demand, the need for more or less output, etc. Rising prices are per se neither good nor bad. They are merely allocating and rationing signals to users and suppliers.

Page 40—*By* JOHN D. HARPER, with which C. WREDE PETERSMEYER has asked to be associated:

Under no circumstances short of full-scale military mobilization can I agree to support a tightening of any elements of the control program. Before irreparable damage occurs to our economy, we ought to begin to relax the program immediately and abandon it entirely as soon as possible.

Page 41—By JOHN D. HARPER:

I fail to see how any Presidential board could have much effect on curbing inflation which has never been caused in any way by actions in the private sector. It can only deal with symptoms of inflation, not causes. Furthermore, I doubt that such a board would have much effect on monetary-fiscal policies which actually cause inflation to get under way.

Page 42—By JOHN R. COLEMAN, with which RICHARD C. FENTON has asked to be associated:

I question both the realism and the wisdom of this goal. We may stretch readers' credulity by setting it out alongside other, more attainable goals and programs. In a growing economy, it is not clear that the costs of moderate inflation (2½%) are of major significance. Any attempt to get below the 2½% figure is all too likely to come at the price of tolerating too much unemployment among its young and its disadvantaged than this society should settle for.

Page 43—By JOSEPH L. BLOCK, with which JOHN D. HARPER has asked to be associated:

While very properly commending the decision to reject profit controls under the existing Phase II programs, the statement is silent on the question of regulating dividends. Although there are no legal controls on dividends, there are guidelines which have served as most effective constraints.

Such action seems inconsistent with the absence of profit controls and it is difficult to fathom the logic of such a move. Surely it is not necessary as a tradeoff for the control of wages since that is accomplished by the regulation of prices. And why are earnings transferred to stockholders as dividends any more inflationary than earnings retained in the business and used to purchase securities, inventory or capital assets?

Such controls deny stockholders their full participation in the profits of a successful enterprise while they suffer the penalties of losing ventures. Furthermore, they appear discriminatory in two respects. They restrict increases of income for such individuals to lower levels than those applicable to wage earners. In addition, they militate against one type of owner—the corporate stockholder—for there are no limitations on the amount of profits an individual proprietor or a partner can take out of a business.

These regulations should be eliminated from the present and any future programs.

Page 43—By HERMAN L. WEISS:

This statement acknowledges the desirability of an expansion in profit *margins* "under some circumstances" but it does not indicate what these circumstances are and what a corporation would have to do to demonstrate that it deserved the opportunity to earn higher profit margins. It would appear from this that allowing business the opportunity to try to increase profit margins would be an exception rather than the rule under the longer term guidelines. I think that exactly the reverse should be the case.

Page 44—By DAVIDSON SOMMERS:

Although I have doubts about several recommendations, my basic reservation is whether the discussion of the need for structural change is sufficiently broad and thorough. Given the unprecedented demands being made on our economy and the inadequacy of public and private mechanisms for making difficult choices in the general interest, I find the discussion of structural change too sketchy and selective. I hope that CED will study this question further, more thoroughly and with a long-term perspective.

Page 45—By ALEXANDER L. STOTT, with which JOHN D. HARPER has asked to be associated:

This statement appears to refer to the service industries only in the narrow or traditional sense of the term. Such service industries as the electric utilities and telephone and telegraph have shown productivity gains that are above the national average.

Page 47—By HERMAN L. WEISS:

I have serious misgivings about advocating "productivity bargaining." Such bargaining is often directed toward the elimination of restrictive work rules. When this is the case, the more restrictive the rules, the greater the wage increases and the faster they come. In such instances, productivity bargaining "rewards the bandits" and, therefore, would be wrong even if it could be confined to the companies and industries with restrictive practices. But it cannot be so confined, because unions which do not have restrictive practices make demands on a comparison basis; then productivity bargaining in one sector generates inflationary bargaining in other sectors.

Page 48—By HERMAN L. WEISS, with which JOHN D. HARPER has asked to be associated:

While I believe there is merit in strengthening the activities of the U.S. Employment Service, I do not believe it should be "federalized" which would undermine the decentralized values of the State Employment Service systems.

Page 49—By ALEXANDER L. STOTT, with which STEWART S. CORT has asked to be associated:

In view of the complexity of the question of the transferability of pension rights and fringe benefits, and the difficulties of implementation, I doubt the desirability of making a recommendation as vague as this one.

Page 50—By HERMAN L. WEISS:

This statement on the "enforcement of the anti-trust laws" is entirely too vague about an area in which there is already a great deal of confusion on the interpretation of these laws.

Page 50—By HERMAN L. WEISS:

The recommendation for "removal of various requirements for price maintenance at retail" is too vague. There is nothing in the report to indicate what is meant by this. I doubt that this is meant to cover Fair Trade or Agency methods of distribution.

Page 51—By PHILIP SPORN:

Whether depression-born or not, one of the strongest of the inflationary biases is the two or three year labor contract entered into in the course of an obvious inflationary cycle which calls for stipulated wage increases in excess of a maximum inflationary limit in the first year and also more or less similar increases fixed for the second and third years. This endorsement of the view

74.

that inflation will continue raises this basic question: How can you expect the next major labor contract negotiated after this particular settlement and approval (piously declared and justified as non-inflationary) to be anything else but an extension and, from labor's mistaken viewpoint, an improvement on the immediately preceding one? How do you stop a fire if you keep on feeding highly flammable fluids into it?

The remedy for this is rather simple. All you have to do is to deny validity to any labor agreement beyond a term of one year which carries a mandatory minimum wage increase in the second and/or succeeding years that is larger than the maximum that can be justified as non-inflationary or than the current rate of annual increase in national productivity at the time of the agreement.

Page 51—By HERMAN L. WEISS, with which JOHN D. HARPER has asked to be associated:

In addition to being ineligible for unemployment compensation, strikers should not be eligible to receive welfare payments, food stamps and surplus commodities, Community Chest and United Fund assistance. A recent study of the Industrial Research Unit, Wharton School of Finance and Commerce, University of Pennsylvania (*Welfare and Strikes: The Use of Public Funds To Support Strikers*) has estimates to indicate that the direct and indirect dollar cost of providing welfare support to strikers will exceed 365 million dollars a year. One of the most important conclusions of the study is that public welfare payments to strikers make strikes last longer, make strike settlements more costly and thus contribute to inflation.

Appendix

Emergency Procedures under the Taft-Hartley and Railway Labor Acts

Under the Taft-Hartley Act, the President can obtain an 80-day injunction prohibiting most threatened or actual nationwide strikes that would in his view imperil national health or safety. If efforts to resolve the dispute during the 80-day "cooling-off" period fail, however, the strike can still take place unless special Congressional action is taken. This procedure is said to have averted crippling strikes in twenty-one out of the twenty-nine cases in which it has been applied since the Act was adopted 26 years ago, and has undoubtedly served as a deterrent to other potential work stoppages. It has, however, proved a notable failure in major strikes involving the longshore and maritime industries. Moreover, in many of the cases where strikes were avoided, the settlements reached were highly inflationary.

A second set of procedures for coping with emergency strikes exists under the Railway Labor Act. This Act applies to both the railroad and the airline industries and can be used on a regional as well as a national basis when there is a threat of a major disruption of essential transportation services. The basic feature of the Act is that when initial mediation efforts have failed, the President can create an Emergency Board to study the dispute and make recommendations for a settlement. For successive 30-day periods during and after the investigations of the Emergency Board, strikes are enjoined but they go into effect thereafter unless special legislation is enacted by the Congress, or the President resorts to such drastic remedies as seizure. Experience under the Act has been quite unsatisfactory. The knowledge that disputes would eventually be turned over to an Emergency Board has generally tended to prevent any genuine collective bargaining prior to the appointment of the Board (there have been 190 emergency boards since the Act was created) and in a growing number of cases, the disputes have eventually been thrown into the lap of Congress.

CED Board of Trustees

as of May 18th

See page 5 for list of Research and Policy Committee and the Subcommittee members who are responsible for the conclusions in this particular study.
as of May 17th

Honorary Trustees

Trustees on Leave for Government Service

CED Professional and Administrative Staff